CROSS ? WORDS
FOR
WIN-WIN

Skills for Resolving Conflict

Shay and Margaret McConnon

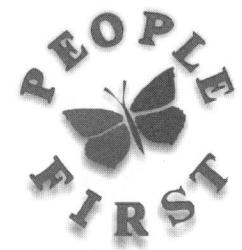

i

First published in Great Britain by People First in 2000
Doves
Highlands Road
Barton on Sea
Hants
BH25 7BL
UK

© Shay and Margaret McConnon 2000

ISBN 0-9538474-0-3

Graphic Layout and Design by
Dave Lovett
Design@graphit.co.uk
www.graphit.co.uk

Printed in Great Britain by
Avalon Design and Print
Christchurch, Dorset

Contents

ACKNOWLEDGEMENTS

Many influences have contributed to the writing of this book. Our thanks to friends and colleagues who have encouraged and supported us in developing the ideas and approaches.

We would like to thank Andy Colehan and John Jerwood for their time, professionalism, friendship and most of all their willingness to challenge.

Our thanks to Dave Lovett who has done a splendid job on the graphics and design of the book. Also to Lesley, his wife, for her tolerance and understanding of late nights and interrupted weekends.

We would like to acknowledge the co-operation, efficiency and general helpfulness of Charlotte Rolfe, our editor.

We are particularly grateful to all the people who have attended our workshops. The shared experiences have contributed greatly to the approaches contained in this book.

We wish to acknowledge all these influences and trust that what is offered in these pages reflects the ideals we share

You and I

I explain quietly. You
hear me shouting. You
try a new tack. I
feel old wounds reopen.

You see both sides. I
see your blinkers. I
am placatory. You
sense a new selfishness.

I am a dove. You
recognise the hawk, You
offer an olive branch. I
feel the thorns.

You bleed. I
see crocodile tears. I
withdraw. You
reel from the impact.

With permission from
Roger McGough

Language for conflict or co-operation ?

Have you ever slammed a door in rage?

Are you inclined to avoid the issue?

Do you say 'you should' or 'you never'?

Do you get the boxing gloves out every time a row beckons?

Do you sometimes make accusing statements like 'you started it' or 'it's your fault'?

Do you often cover up your real feelings by saying 'it doesn't matter' when it does, or 'I'm fine' when you are not ?

Ever been so hurt, angry and resentful that you don't care about the other person, you just want revenge?

Have you ever wished you could handle those difficult people better?

Use words wisely.

If so, then this book is for you. It will give you some tried and proven ways to prevent and manage conflict in your life. It is written for parents, managers, teachers, students, anyone who wishes to manage differences in open and honest ways without argument or conflict.

Me and my big mouth!

No matter who you are, or where you live, if you are in contact with other people you are likely to face some form of conflict, be it a minor irritation or an earth-shattering row.

The answer to resolving these conflicts is right under your nose, in the words you use. Cross words can cause your conflict – rearrange the words to resolve it. Words enable you to build bridges or create barriers. Words have the power to

☞ heal or wound.
☞ unite or divide.
☞ create conflict or harmony.

The cost of conflict

Of course we are all different from each other. We have different needs, tastes, opinions, beliefs, preferences and values. The question is, how do we cope with the differences? Are they allowed to get in the way and be the source of conflict, or can we celebrate the differences and view them creatively? Let's look at a few problem scenarios.

Relationship cost

Kate finds Pete increasingly distant and hostile at times. She would like to come home from work and chat about her day and hear all about his day, but he comes home wanting to be left alone to unwind. Kate feels excluded, and Pete seems to be spending more and more time in front of his computer.

Conflict wastes time and money.

What needs to happen? Would a good row clear the air? Should they pretend there isn't a problem? What choices do they have? What are the words they need to use to resolve this difference?

Family cost

It's the second time this week – Lisa wanting to stay out till one in the morning with her teenage friends, Dad insisting she be in at eleven.

The increasing tension and anger shows in the raised voices: *'You're just old fashioned ... all my friends' parents let them stay out late.'*

'This is my house and while I pay the mortgage, you'll go along with my rules.'

As Lisa slams the door, Dad shakes his head in despair and wonders what can he can do. This is an example of people talking themselves into trouble. What choices do Lisa and her dad have for talking themselves out of trouble?

Cost to the individual

While conflict can be constructive, most conflict is destructive, with time, emotional and health costs. Kate and Pete, Lisa and her dad might argue, retaliate, blame and engage in a war of words. Such power struggles can result in stress, loss of confidence, unhappiness, hostility, withdrawal and even illness.

Cost to the organisation

Conflict not only has a high personal cost but it is expensive for your organisation. Research indicates that a typical manager loses 25% of the day responding to unhelpful conflict. This is time lost to creative, productive work.

Take a medium sized organisation with one hundred managers. Let's assume the average annual salary per manager is £40,000. With managers losing 25% of their time on conflict, the cost will be £1,000,000.

3

This only accounts for management time. The true cost will include wasted employee time, higher staff turnover, missed opportunities, absenteeism, inefficiency, low morale and poor teamwork.

Conversely of course, people who are skilled at managing conflict are more likely to be perceived as leaders, are more influential, gain respect and co-operation and increase the worth of an organisation.

Unmanaged conflict is the largest reducible cost for many organisations and it is usually the least recognised.

Breaking the stalemate

In conflict, there is the danger that people get locked into their own positions, digging their heels in and insisting they get their own way. If this happens, it is stalemate with both sets of needs unmet. It is a *you against me* scenario.

This book is about how to make the transformation from *you against me* to *us against the problem*. It is about giving the reader more behavioural choices in managing differences. It will leave you better equipped to deal with the difficult people in your life. It will show you how to

☞ prevent blow-ups.
☞ defuse anger.
☞ build bridges.
☞ keep your cool.
☞ resolve conflict for good.
☞ build better relationships.
☞ avoid the pitfalls.

Chapter overview

The first chapter in this book recognises that each of us has our unique window on the world, which is likely to be one-sided, distorted and subjective. This will explain why we are different from, and difficult for, each other.

Chapter 2 suggests that conflict comes more from the management of these differences than from the differences themselves.

Chapter 3 explores win-lose and win-win mind sets and the consequences of these approaches.

Chapter 4 gives some practical ways to defuse your own anger and to manage the feelings of others.

Chapter 5 shows you how to listen acceptingly, talk constructively and negotiate successfully. You will also learn how to disagree and keep rapport.

Chapter 6 gives you the language and the processing for win-win. These 'steps' will enable you to manage differences in open and honest ways without conflict or argument.

Chapter 7 shows you how to nip conflict in the bud. Discover ways to deal with the irritations and minor tensions rather than letting them fester.

In the appendices there is a questionnaire to help you discover your preferred conflict management style and a collection of other tools to help you to turn difficult situations around.

The four-step model outlined in Chapter 6 has evolved through work on conflict management in organisations and couple counselling. The approach is designed to reduce defensiveness, deepen understanding, create collaboration and lead to mutual problem-solving.

How the view explains our differences

Without realising it, we can become stuck in how we view
things. The first way we look at something is not always
the only or the 'best' way. The more ways we can view
a situation, the more possibilities we will discover and the
more creative we can be.

Where do you see this circle:

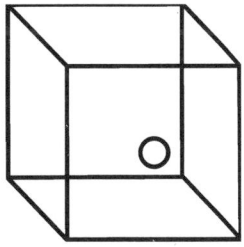

at the lower right hand corner of
the rear panel?

at the centre of the front panel?

at the lower right corner of the
front panel?

at the centre of the back panel?

Different views

An old story tells how five blind men once went to find out
what an elephant was like. They found one and felt it all over.
One found its waving trunk. 'It's like a snake,' he said.

Another found its tail. 'More like a rope,' was his opinion.

A third touched one of the elephant's big ears. 'It's like a
fan,' he said.

'No, like a pillar,' said the fourth, feeling its great leg.

The last man leaned against the elephant's massive side.
'It's like a wall,' he declared.

Each of them experienced the elephant from his own point of view, and each came to a different conclusion. That is the trouble with points of view. If you want a true view of anything, you must look at it from every angle. Otherwise, if you stick to your own point of view, as someone has said, you will sit on the point and lose the view.

We all have slightly different views on the world. Our window on the world is filtered by our early experiences, beliefs and memories. These filters allow us to deal with the two million bits of information that we are exposed to at any one moment. It is impossible to process all this data. So we delete, distort and generalise the incoming information.

Beware of expecting others to see what you see.

However, many of us believe that the way we experience the world is the way it is. It is your unique view … it is the truth for you. Others will have a different view. Their truth, while being different from yours, is right for them.

Your reality is not totality

Of course we don't have totality. What we experience is subjective, partial and likely to be distorted. People believed the world was flat until fifteenth-century explorers discovered that we can go to the East by sailing west. When Albert Einstein was ten years old, his teacher told him that he would not amount to much. Mr Gottlieb Daimler, the founder of Daimler Motor Company, said that the car would never catch on because there would never be enough chauffeurs. The president of Decca Records, rejecting the Beatles, said, 'We don't like their sound and guitar music is on the way out anyway.'

Which person is the tallest?

Our views are always restricted to the window we have on our world and its filters. Without realising it, we are discounting something from what is out there.

How much can you trust your experiences?

Is the world flat? Well it certainly looks it. Is it stationary? It has that appearance. However, the astronomer will tell us we are rotating at thousands of miles an hour. Is the chair you are sitting on solid? If I strike my hand against it, it certainly feels solid. However, the physicist will tell us it is a moving bundle of energy.

Difficult people

Who is this person? Is he quick to act, rash or abrasive? He is all three, it depends on the window and the view. They are opinions, each one created from a partial view with information discounted. Who is right? Everyone and no one.

A bucket of water can be a home to a fish, a cool drink to an elephant and a lake to an ant. What you experience reflects who you are. If someone is difficult for you, how much does that reflect you? There will be other people who won't find that behaviour difficult ... they have a different window on it. Maybe people are difficult because of who you are!

Who is right?

Fox-hunting is a sport to some people and slaughter to another. Everyone thinks he is right, and each opinion will be right for that individual. There is always more than what any of us are noticing at any given moment. Expand your view to grow in wisdom.

Can you see the hero?

Because you don't see something, it doesn't mean it is not there. Even though you can't see the stars when the sun comes up, they are still there. You might see this person as abrasive. Behind abrasiveness is quickness to act; this is a strength, even though you might not see it as such. Every villain is likely to be a hero in his own story.

Recognise the positive intention

Conflict often comes from goodwill, people thinking they are doing right but in fact getting it wrong. Having been round the block three times looking for a street, you suggest to your partner that he stops and asks someone ... and the advice is rejected. Although you were only trying to help, your partner heard an attack on his competence.

I care - you feel smothered
I am assertive - you see me as aggressive
I am principled - you experience me as stubborn
I am ambitious - you see me as ruthless

Intent and impact

We are inclined to draw conclusions about people's intentions from how their behaviour impacts on us. I feel hurt, therefore you intended to hurt me. I feel put down, so your intention was to humiliate me.

This is not always the case. When someone says *'But I was only trying to help you'* they are really saying they have a positive intention, even though your experience of it was negative.

Beware of making assumptions about people's intentions. You may wish to assume the best about the person, not the worst. In his view he is a hero. Acknowledge this, *'I appreciate you want to help, however, I feel smothered and in future I would like to ... '* Now there is the possibility that real understanding and collaboration will ensue.

State your positive intention

Ask yourself what is your real purpose in what you are about to say or do. *'I don't want to waste your time and I'd like to clear up some misunderstandings ...'* To enhance co-operation, tell your truth in a way that the other recognises your positive intention.

Watch your language

While I experience you as abrasive, to say *'You are abrasive'* is unhelpful and likely to lead to argument, as it is not how you see yourself. The view through your window is *'I am quick to act.'*

'You' language is likely to be confrontational. Talk about what you experience about the other person through your window ... and don't expect them to have the same view as you!

Do say

> *My view is …*
> *My perception is …*
> *What I experience is …*
> *What I need is …*
> *My concerns are …*

Beware

> *You never …*
> *You are …*
> *You should …*

Opinions or facts?

In the film *Annie Hall*, Alvie Singer complains

'We never have sex'.

'We're constantly having sex', says his girlfriend.

'How often do you have sex?', asks the therapist.

'Three times a week', they reply in unison.

In conflict we are inclined to treat opinions as if they are facts. Opinions are not right or wrong, they are points of view. They are what you are noticing through that window of yours, which of course, is different to what others are noticing through their windows. Having sex three times a week is a fact. Whether that is too much or too little, is an opinion.

Truth or importance?

> *You drive too fast.*
> *I deserve a pay rise.*

Don't argue with perception.

These opinions are not about what is true but what is important to you. If different things are important to you, these opinions of mine will seem a nonsense and we will just argue. When arguing, I am convinced that I am right and this only distracts me from exploring your world. It is not whether one view is right and another wrong, it is that both views matter. One view is seldom enough.

People who run with the mind set *'I am right'* will be inclined to see others as the problem and that *they* should change … they are the ones who are being unreasonable, closed and stubborn. In reality, it is the arrogance of the 'I am right' attitude that is likely to perpetuate the problem.

Changing someone

Trying to change someone rarely results in change. Change is more likely to come from understanding. Wanting to change someone implies there is something wrong with that person and of course this only leads to defensiveness and argument. Seeking to understand, suggests the other person is OK in her view of the world. This is the mind set that creates collaboration and mutual problem-solving.

Blame

Blame looks to the past and who was right or wrong. You may wish to keep the focus on the future and how the situation can be solved. When your dog goes missing, where is the energy better spent … looking for the dog or arguing over who left the gate open? When we feel accused, we can spend the time in futile arguing rather than productive problem-solving. Avoid making the other person wrong.

Sense and nonsense

When we argue, we tend to offer our opinions, use 'shoulds' and give advice.

> *You should be more considerate.*
> *Slow down.*
> *If only you wouldn't be so selfish.*

These opinions and advice are like the tip of the iceberg of your thinking. Underneath, and unseen, will be your experiences, beliefs and concerns, from which you form these opinions and advice. They make total sense to you.

However, to someone with a different set of experiences, beliefs and values they become nonsense. Of course, this person will offer different opinions and advice in line with their values, beliefs and experiences.

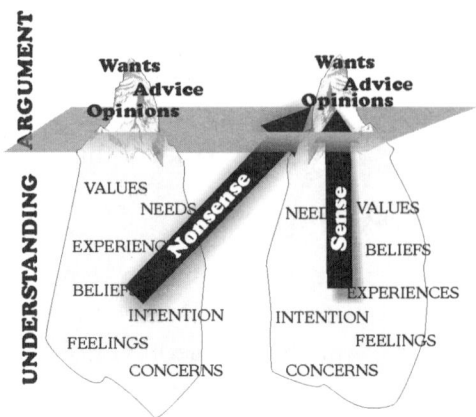

When we argue, we are likely to be at the tip of the iceberg, trading in the surface thinking of opinions and 'shoulds'.

Understanding is about exploring the unseen bits of other people's icebergs, their thoughts, feelings and intentions. It's about exploring information on themselves that they have access to but that you don't yet see. Arguing drives people apart, understanding draws people together. Rather than contradict a view, you might wish to add to it.

Explore different perspectives for richer solutions.

Fight the difference or celebrate it?

Every day in the media we hear or read about war, violence, divorce and social unrest. Talk to your friends and they will tell you about their rows, arguments and difficult people. Your children will argue over the TV and you may even have experienced road rage.

Some people see conflict as a game, a combat sport and they look for sparring partners. Others can be devastated by the merest tiff.

Is conflict inevitable? Is a relationship without conflict healthy? Is harmony even desirable? Is conflict always bad and to be avoided?

The differences don't have to get in the way.

Is conflict inevitable?

Conflict is not inevitable simply because we are different. We can disagree and not be in conflict. Conflict is more to do with style than substance. It happens because of what we do and say about the differences, rather than arising from the differences themselves.

Conflict starters

The escalation or diffusion of conflict is to do with style, the words and the emotional energy used. Here are some ways that escalate conflict.

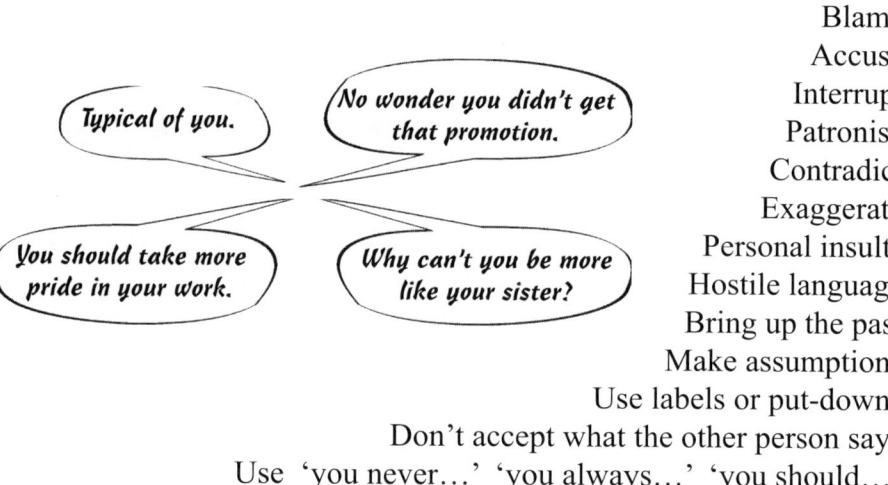

Typical of you.

No wonder you didn't get that promotion.

You should take more pride in your work.

Why can't you be more like your sister?

Blame
Accuse
Interrupt
Patronise
Contradict
Exaggerate
Personal insults
Hostile language
Bring up the past
Make assumptions
Use labels or put-downs
Don't accept what the other person says
Use 'you never…' 'you always…' 'you should…'

Circumstances can escalate the conflict

Issues that are resolved in minutes on that sunny beach in the middle of that relaxed holiday, can turn out very differently if you both have had a hard day, it is late in the evening and the children won't settle!

Things that can turn a trivial issue into a major disagreement include:

☞ tiredness
☞ stress
☞ insecurity
☞ illness
☞ mood
☞ alcohol

Conflict is complex

We might be arguing about money but the real issue may be about control. That sloppy report which is handed in late might be to do with a lack of recognition and a feeling of being taken for granted.

When a minor incident erupts into a major row, there is likely to be a deeper, more complex issue at stake. The screwdriver left in the wrong place, the toothpaste squeezed in the middle, the car parked at an angle ... suddenly you feel you have walked on a landmine – you probably have! The row is not about the screwdriver or the car but a deeper unfulfilled need ... perhaps to be valued, to be involved, to be accepted.

As the issue is hidden, we may not be conscious of what it is that is upsetting us until we talk about it. Until people talk about and discover the underlying need, they will be dealing with the symptoms, patching things up, becoming more frustrated and growing apart.

Little hurts

Have you ever noticed how a small graze or cut finger can really hurt when you brush against someone? Without the sore, it would have gone unnoticed. When life is going well, we also have a buffer, which protects us in the small 'brushes' with life. If the little conflicts of life hurt deeply, it may be useful to notice any other sore or deeper issue. Deal with causes not symptoms.

Is conflict constructive?

Many people suggest that conflict is healthy and constructive. While conflict can provide broader perspectives and deeper understanding, for most people conflict is destructive.

A conflict is constructive only if as a result

☞ the relationship is stronger.
☞ you understand each other more.
☞ there is greater willingness to meet each other's needs.
☞ there is greater trust.
☞ you have resolved the source of future conflicts.
☞ there are richer perspectives.

If the conflict results in deeper frustration, negative feelings and a growing hostility, it is destructive to the relationship. You have created a remedial situation from which you have to recover.

How rows can spiral out of control

We don't always see a row brewing. It can catch us unawares. Before you know it, a spark becomes a flame, then a fire, and you don't seem to be able to control it any more.

A slight difference over weekend plans can lead to personal insults, widen to include an attack on in-laws, and suddenly the couple are ready to break up.

It is OK to be different, it is not OK to dysfunction.

(Pete arrives home late from work and tired after a long day).

Kate: Where have you been? You didn't say you'd be late.

Pete: I don't have to account for every minute of my time.

Kate: This is typical, you never consider anyone else.

Pete: You are getting more and more like your mother, nag nag nag ... I wonder why I come home at all.

Kate: So do I ... you just sit in front of the computer expecting to be waited on hand and foot.

Pete: You haven't got a clue.

Kate: You know what your problem is ...

(Pete storms out, slamming the door and shouting).

Road to breakdown

Here are some stages that relationships go through on the way to breakdown.

1 Discussion

This is when both people are interested in the other's view of the world and are prepared to share ideas, opinions and feelings. This stage is simply the meeting of minds with no intention to get the other person to think or feel anything different.

Characteristics include:

☞ respect for each other's viewpoint
☞ acceptance of the other's values
☞ broadening of perspectives

2 Debate

This is when there are different viewpoints and I would like you to see things my way, but only if it is right for you.

Characteristics include:

☞ openness to your ideas
☞ respect for your viewpoint

3 Argument

I want you to 'buy' my ideas, regardless of what you may be thinking. I am 'right' and you are 'wrong'. You should be doing it my way.

Characteristics include:

☞ disregard for other's viewpoint
☞ arguing from own perspective only
☞ polarisation
☞ lots of 'yes buts ...'

4 Conflict

Not only do I believe I am 'right' and you are 'wrong' but I insist you do it my way that you act according to my values and beliefs.

Characteristics include:

☞ demands that you behave, as I want
☞ highly personalised arguments
☞ lots of 'shoulds'
☞ blame, accusation, put-downs

5 Breakdown

The relationship is now so painful that I need to protect myself or recover from the pain. I act as if you don't exist.

Characteristics include:

☞ silence
☞ cold war
☞ separate lives

How far through these stages do you need to go to manage differences in open and honest ways? You may find that argument and beyond are signposts to broken rapport and a deteriorating relationship.

What are the choices?

Each of us is different and special. We have our unique beliefs, values and needs. Different perspectives, viewpoints, goals and approaches are the natural consequence of these differences. The greater the differences, the more difficult it can become to maintain harmony in the relationship.

We have three broad choices when it comes to managing differences.

1　We can choose to discuss and debate our differences, respecting each other's opinion.
2　We can argue about these differences, i.e. we are convinced we are right and the other should have our perspective.
3　We can move into conflict about these differences by imposing our way of doing things.

What drives the conflict?

David delegates to Michael in a detailed, precise way, insisting he follow the procedures that he has decided are right. Michael feels restricted and performs best when he can be creative. He likes to be given a task and the freedom on how to complete it.

Argument

They argue. David argues that getting the job done right means that procedures are agreed and followed. Michael argues that procedures can restrict creativity and demotivate him. In essence David wants something that Michael doesn't value and vice versa.

Conflict

Why do you insist on me seeing what you see, when I don't?

Arguing is 'intellectual'. Conflict is behavioural. Conflict happens when David insists his procedures are followed, preventing Michael from operating in a way that is important to him. This is a violation of Michael's needs. The consequence is that Michael will begin to feel *worth less,* be unhappy and less motivated.

Arrogance

While difference lies at the source of this conflict – David needs procedures and Michael needs to be creative – it is arrogance that drives the conflict. Each is convinced he is 'right', *his* way is best and the other 'should' be like him. If the other person was like you, had your beliefs, values and way of doing things you wouldn't be in conflict. The sub text around conflict is: *'I want you like me ... you should be like me.' 'I want you to change to me, my ways, my standards.'*

> You are creating the conflict in your life if you are imposing your values on others, denying them, their needs.
>
> Others are creating the conflict in your life if they are imposing their values on you, denying you, your needs.

We may not recognise that we are denying other people their needs. We are likely to have a positive intention and are doing what we consider 'right' and best.

Reduce the conflict in your life by imposing less.

Rules, expectations and 'shoulds'

If I make value judgements – 'you should' 'you ought' 'you must', I am implying that my way is best for you, that my values are more important than yours. This is both arrogant and disrespectful … it is not accepting that the other person can legitimately value other things.

I expect you to notice my feelings.

I expect you to consult me.

We are inclined to expect others to value what we value. Procedures are important to David and he expects Michael to value these too. Our expectations follow on our values and become our 'rules' for life.

I expect you to listen to me.

When my expectations are not met, when my rules are broken, we are in conflict.

23

Beware of the 'should'

If I believe my boss should support me in front of others,
I will be in conflict with him if he criticises me in front of
my work colleagues. The conflict is happening because of a
mismatch between his behaviour and what I expect it should
be. Someone who expects the boss to be straightforward in
public, if necessary, has different expectations
and will not be in conflict because of
that behaviour.

Reduce conflict by recognising the positive intention.

Whose rules are right?

Your rules are right ... they are right for
you, they show the way to meeting your needs and getting
what is important to you. But what is important to you won't
be for others, their rules are right for them. What will be
'wrong' is to impose your rules on other people and expect
them to live by your rules.

Win-lose is when both people are trying to have their needs
met at the expense of the other person's. *Win-win* is when
both people problem-solve so all needs are met.

Who knows best?

While each of us is 'right' in expecting and needing different
things, it is sometimes necessary for an experienced person
(boss, parent, or teacher) to determine what is in the other's
best interests. This is best when discussion of needs has
taken place and an understanding shown for each other's
positions.

When Barry was fifteen years old, he wanted to leave school
and work as a car mechanic. His father had a different view,
he wanted him to go to university. It took some time for
Barry to see a different perspective but now he is glad that
his father persisted. Today he is the vice-president of a multi-
national corporation.

Resolving conflict

As conflict is caused by a denial of people's needs, the successful resolution must result in the satisfaction of those needs, otherwise the conflict could simmer and re-ignite. If you want a lasting win, look for the win for the other.

If Michael just ignored David's need for procedures and does the work his way, his needs are met and David's are not ... it is *win-lose*, 10 for Michael and 0 for David. If David pulls rank and insists that Michael follow his procedures regardless of his need to be creative, this is *lose-win*, 0 for Michael and 10 for David.

In both these scenarios the conflict remains unresolved and will continue, albeit under the surface, until there is some element of *win-win*.

Conflict resolved in the unshaded area is likely to keep re-emerging as needs are largely still unmet. Try to get a compromise with 5/5 and above. While it may not be possible to get 100% satisfaction, aim for at least 50% + satisfaction for both parties.

Celebrate the difference

The view through your window is different, not better, not right, just different. You are OK and I am OK. The difference need not be the battleground, it can be the source for broader perspectives. There is nothing wrong with you and there is nothing wrong with me, but there may be something wrong between us. Celebrate rather than fight the difference.

**While differences explain conflict,
it is arrogance that drives it.**

Are you building a bridge or a barrier?

Conflict will escalate or defuse because of your conflict management style. How you respond impacts on the result you get. Whether you defend, attack, retreat, appease, you affect how the other will respond. It is a dynamic moment and you control the direction and the final outcome by the processes you use … by how you use your words and energy.

Does this happen?

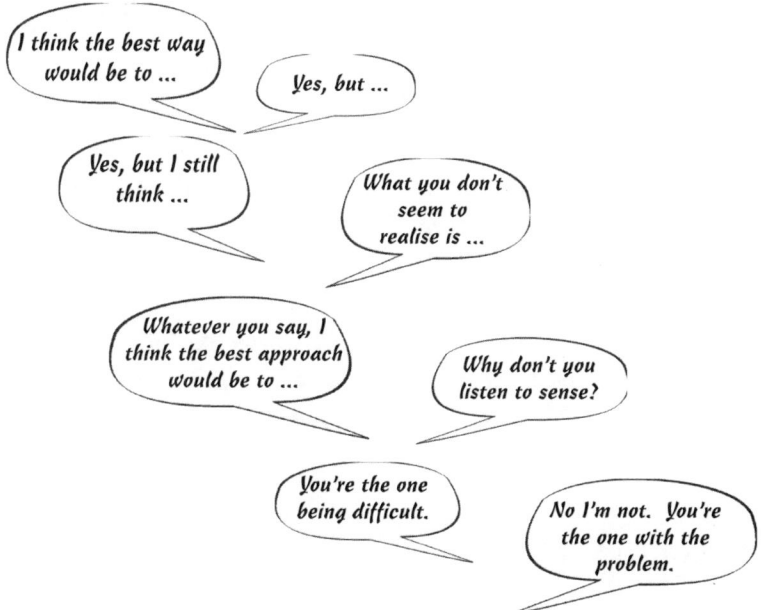

You and me becoming we

To the extent that you are able to translate *me* and *you* into *we*, you will develop affinity, rapport and get co-operation. If you don't, there is the real likelihood of division, frustration and the escalation of conflict.

In conflict, people usually feel under threat of losing something which is important to them. It is this perceived threat that puts them on the defensive and there is little chance of getting collaboration while it remains. A joint solution is more likely to be achieved if the threat, real or imaginary, is removed. To achieve this, focus on the other person with the intent to meet their needs. Attending to what you want, regardless of the other, can create this threat.

There is nothing to be gained from attacking the other person and everything to lose.

The resolution mind set

It doesn't have to be win-lose. If I win £10, you lose £10. If I have three quarters of the cake, you will only have a quarter. If one person gets the promotion, the other loses out. This win-lose mind set forces you into a competitive attitude and language.

This mind set is appropriate in sports but can miss the point where people are concerned. The win-lose tactic assumes there is not enough for everyone to have what he or she needs. Lisa wants to be in at one in the morning and Dad wants her home by eleven. These times exclude each other. As we shall see later in the book, shifting the perspective from wants to needs, can provide a lot more flexibility in terms of win-win.

A reluctant partner

People often get in their own way.

It takes two to be in conflict and it requires the will of two to resolve the conflict. If you find that the other party is not interested in resolving the conflict, but wants to hurt or win at any cost, then a different approach is necessary. You may need to protect yourself from the conflict, to walk away or to seek a third party intervention.

To get a more co-operative response you may want to look at how you are perceived. Are you seen as a threat? Are people suspicious of your motives? While this may not be how you see yourself, it could be how you are perceived. You might be OK but others may not see you as OK.

Try a positive statement. Mention your intention. Ask what is needed from you. Talk about the advantage for the other person.

> *I would like to find a solution that works for both of us.*
> *How do you suggest we go about this?*

However, some people will have more to gain by keeping the problem alive than by solving it. Hence they will be reluctant to work with you.

Cross words

When winning becomes more important than understanding, it's a *you versus me* scenario. Then, instead of listening, people are likely to be preparing a counter-argument or even a counter-attack!

The win-lose mind set leaks out in the language used. It can become a war of words with lots of verbal bullets.

> *Any fool knows …*
> *Of all the stupid ideas …*
> *The trouble with you is …*
> *You must be an idiot if you can't see …*

If you shoot from the hip, you could end up with a bullet in your foot.

To get more fire-power, we attack the person *'No wonder you have been passed over for promotion four times.'* When we need some heavy weaponry we bring out some old mortar bombs *'... and it was your fault that we lost the PX contract.'* Hostile language eats up large amounts of time without achieving anything.

People can get locked into hostile language patterns. It is as if they know no other way of approaching differences. People who use co-operative language are likely to bridge the differences. Hostile language opens the divide and creates division. Keep the language environment clean if you want people to act from their heads rather than their stomachs. It was Benjamin Franklin who said that any fool can criticise, condemn and complain … and most fools do.

Some people are great at continuing to do what doesn't work.

Conflict must be fuelled

People may get into hostility loops, feeding more ammunition and pain into the loop from both directions … both are struggling for power and are locked into the win-lose mind set. The gap widens and each digs himself into a deeper hole.

Hostility loops have to be fed, they are not self-sustaining. It takes two to argue but only one to stop ... without fuel for the loop, the hostility will splutter and the emotional intensity weaken.

Bridging

You can argue till you are 'blue in the face' but you will lose if you make the other person feel outdone. You can outtalk, outsmart, outwit, outreason but still fail, if the other person does not feel good at the end. Only if the other person's needs are heard and met will it be a win. You win when he wins.

30

The person you are in conflict with is likely to be more interested in what he needs and wants than in what you need or want.

Bridging is about attending to that person, noticing the needs, concerns and feelings, finding common ground, finding places where *you* and *I* can become *we*, where interests, needs and concerns can be seen as mutual. The more communication you invite, the more you are likely to create the win-win environment. This can be done verbally and non-verbally.

Don't expect others to collaborate if you go on the attack.

Bridge mind set

**You are OK
Let's work together
I want us both to win
I want power with you
Your needs are important
Let's problem-solve rather than argue
We have a mutual problem to be solved**

Some bridging words

**Us
We
Our
Can
Let's talk
Appreciate
Alternatives
What do you need?
What do you think?
Help me understand
What would you say to...?**

Non-verbals

Soft gestures
Open posture
Make eye contact
Voice low and slow
Look and act approachable
Sit or stand at angle of approximately 90°
Use open hand gestures – palms slightly upturned

Barrier mind-set

Fight the problem, not the person.

I am right
You should change
You are the problem
I want power over you
I want to lay down the law
I want to prove you wrong
I am indifferent to your needs
You are wrong and you should be different
My needs are more important than yours are

Some barrier words

Me
You should
Waste of time
Your problem is
That won't work
Out of the question
That's my final word
This is non-negotiable
You don't understand
I've heard all this before
You wouldn't understand

ME
ME
Win - lose

Non-verbals

Frowning
Lip-biting
Raised voice
Arms crossed
Hands on hips
Sharp gestures
Hands in pockets
Hands over mouth
Avoiding eye contact
Narrowing of the eyes

Be partners, rather than opponents.

Power with, not over

To share power does not mean giving up power. It can be like sharing the light of a candle. When you light another person's candle, your light does not diminish. In fact there is more light for everyone.

The enlightened approach to resolving conflict involves respect. Respect is about recognising others as being different and accepting them with their differences. It happens when I am able to say *You're OK* even though you have a different set of values and principles from me ... if I accept you for who you are rather than who I want you to be ... if I recognise that your needs, although different, are as important as mine.

Win-win is more likely when people

- ☞ focus on both sets of needs, concerns and feelings.
- ☞ respect each other's view.
- ☞ see the issue as a mutual problem to be solved.
- ☞ are prepared to listen and compromise.
- ☞ are not interested in winning at any cost.
- ☞ opt for power with rather than power over.

The power of co-operation

People will not co-operate with you, if you seem to be against them. Aim to be open, receptive and willing to collaborate.

Create an atmosphere in which everyone feels that something can be gained, i.e. everyone is a winner. Maybe you don't get what you want until others get what they want.

For me to win, you don't have to lose.

Understand and manage your feelings

Have you ever been so hurt, angry and resentful that you don't care about the other person, you don't even want to resolve the conflict, you just want to get revenge and to hurt? Even 'nice' people can become abusive and threatening in conflict.

Unresolved feelings have a habit of leaking into the conversation. Even when you desperately try not to let your emotions show, they can pop like the cork from a champagne bottle, often with messy results. How can you control these feelings and what can you do to prevent the anger?

While feelings are OK, there will be feelings you don't want.

Recognise the anger

Feelings are indicators of what is going on in your life. Anger is a signal that something is not right for you. It is your body's way of letting you know that something is wrong, that your values have been violated. Feelings are just another part of you, like your arms and legs and like your arms and legs, they can be controlled.

Venting

While you may have a strong urge to shout, scream, kick, hit or run, acting out of the anger is likely to be destructive to a collaborative relationship. Beware of what you say in the heat of anger. The cross words could constitute the best speech you will ever regret!

Playing your personal stereo at high volume will cause hearing loss of the higher frequencies. Yelling and shouting is also likely to result in hearing loss ... the other person may just 'close down'. A soft and gentle tonality is likely to improve hearing. You may wish to try speaking about your anger rather than speaking from your anger. People who throw temper tantrums are usually not taken seriously.

Suppressing

Anger that is not dealt with can turn inwards and leak out in resentment, bitterness, withdrawal and depression. Suppressed negative feelings can damage your health. While it is easy to suggest you describe and express your anger in a positive way to the relevant person, experience may have taught you it is expedient to settle for surface peace as the lesser of two evils.

Unexpressed conflict is still conflict.

Releasing

Suppressed anger is stored in the body. If it is not released it can build to the point where you 'explode' or 'dump' on someone. Find a way that is right for you to manage your stress, otherwise it will act as a toxin to your system and can lead to illness and disease. Talking with friends, sports, meditation, relaxation can all be ways of releasing the stress.

Some people need space to think before they are ready to discuss a conflict. Some need to sort it out quickly. Respect each other's needs and agree a time to talk. Allowing issues to accumulate can add fuel to growing anger.

> *I was angry with my friend*
> *I told my wrath, my wrath did end.*
> *I was angry with my foe*
> *I told it not, my wrath did grow.*
>
> **William Blake**

Manage your anger

Conflict is often high on emotion and low on reasoning. When the anger 'runs' me, essentially I become more stupid, in the sense that my perspective narrows. I become less rational. The primitive part of the brain takes over. I can't think clearly. I am likely to do and say things I will regret later.

> *Anger can severely limit your choices.*

When you get angry, adrenaline flows faster, veins are enlarged, your heart beats faster. The body is equipped for a brawl rather than for problem-solving. Where do these feelings come from and what can you do about them?

How do you 'do' feelings?

Whatever you feel, you have a strategy for it. Feelings are a consequence of something you do. Your anger will be related to your thinking, your body and your language. Make an intervention in one or all three areas and you will change the feeling.

Feelings are less to do with the 'real' world and more to do with what you tell yourself about the 'real' world. It is all to do with that unique, subjective, partial view you have.

It is the middle of the night and you hear the floorboards creaking … you are convinced a burglar is creeping up the stairs and you feel terrified. Your feelings are unfounded however, as it was only the stair boards contracting after a warm summer's day.

> *As you see the world in new ways, your feelings will shift.*

On another occasion, you again hear the stair boards creaking and you tell yourself that it is only the boards contracting … and you feel calm, even though this time there really is a prowler on the stairs!

Watch your thinking

Feelings follow on from your thoughts. Change your thinking if you want to change your feelings. The thinking behind anger is likely to contain a *'you should'*.

> ***You should*** *be more considerate.*

> ***You should*** *have known.*

Take the *'you should'* out of the thinking and how angry can you be?

> *Being considerate was a choice he had.*

Remember, *'you shoulds'* imply that my way is best for you, that my values, beliefs and methodologies are better than yours. By taking the *'you should'* out of your thinking, you can inoculate yourself from anger.

Guilt comes from *'I should'*.

> ***I should*** *have helped more.*

Forgive others for your sake.

Take the *'I should'* out and how guilty can you feel?

And of course, you run the risk of causing resentment when you tell others what *'they should'* do. Simple as it seems, by taking the *'shoulds'* out of your internal and external conversations, you reduce anger, guilt and resentment.

You may wish to replace *'shoulds'* with *'coulds'*. Rather than say *'I should'* try *'I could'*. Instead of saying *'you should'* use *'you could'* or *'I need'*.

Watch your physiology

Your anger will be reflected in your physiology, your gestures and your voice. It is as if your body contains the anger. Try to be angry without clenched teeth, a high-pitched voice or wagging your forefinger, and you could discover that you can't get as angry. Note how your body is when you are angry and reverse this, e.g. if you find yourself pointing with your right forefinger, next time put your right hand in your pocket and point with your left hand.

Reverse the expression and you diminish the feeling.

Anger is fuelled by your thinking, your body and your language.

Suggestions for next time:

☞ Lower the volume of your voice.
☞ Slow the rate of speaking.
☞ Use circular rather than linear gestures.
☞ Breathe from the stomach.
☞ Soften the face muscle.
☞ Delay before responding.

Watch your language

Your anger is somehow contained not only in your physiology but also in your language. Rearrange the cross words for a different experience. Instead of saying *'I'm pi**ed off'* try *'I'm annoyed with you'* or *'I'm disappointed.'* It is as if the anger is in the words, and if I choose less expressive language, I will experience less anger.

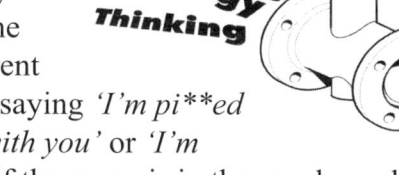

Coping with anger in others

What do you do when the other person is shouting and screaming at you? While you may need to protect yourself from anger that is directed at you, recognise that some people need to let off steam before they can begin to move forward. Rather than going on instinct by retaliating or retreating, listen and encourage the venting. In this way you are likely to defuse the hostility and get to calmness and rationality.

'Brake time'

If you validate, listen and paraphrase and yet the other person remains accusatory and abusive, you may wish to separate yourself. It takes two to play. If you don't have a partner you don't have a game! Avoid running or storming out of the situation. Excuse yourself: *'I recognise you have strong feelings about this and I think it would be best if we talk about this after we have had a chance to think things through.'*

> If both of you are yelling, no one is in charge.

When an argument is getting out of hand, you may wish to take a break for half an hour or so to 'cool' down.

'I feel this is getting us nowhere ... I'm getting too worked up here ... would it be a good idea to take a break and meet again at three o'clock?'

It takes two to fight, one to stop. The bottling up of anger and walking out of the room in a 'huffed' silence is not brake time. Nor is avoiding the conflict, brake time. By giving yourselves time, you take the 'heat' out of the situation to confront the issues more rationally. Brake time is about postponing the talking, not avoiding it. Defuse the anger to deal with the problem.

What not to do

Avoid giving advice or telling the other person to do anything ... this is likely to make them angrier and cause resentment.

> Calm down ...

> There's no need to be so angry ...

> Keep your voice down ...

The sub text in these responses is 'you are wrong to be angry'. Such an invalidation will break rapport.

> Validate the feeling to keep rapport.

What to do

1 Validate

Acknowledge what the other person is feeling and recognise it as valid for her.

> *I can see you have strong feelings about this.*
> *So you feel ... because ...*

2 Ask the magic question 'what ... ?'

By asking the person what they want you are giving them some control and reducing the feeling of helplessness ... you are creating a *power with* scenario and the need for anger is dissipating.

> *What do you need from me?*
> *What needs to happen ...?*

> People who say sorry don't always forgive.

3 Check for understanding

Paraphrase to ensure you understand what the person has said. It is difficult to continue to be angry when someone is genuinely trying to understand you.

> *So what you are saying is ...*
> *If I understand you correctly ...*

Listening is key

Listen without interrupting, arguing or disagreeing. Accept what they say as their reality. It is their perception, it is valid for them while it may not coincide with your perception.

Listen to understand even if there is blame, accusation or demand, even if as you see it, there are distortions and exaggerations.

Listening leads to understanding, and understanding is the foundation for agreement. Conflict grows in the absence of understanding.

Listening is key to making the transformation from *you against me* to *us against the problem*.

Chapter 5
Skills

It's a warm summer's afternoon and the fly in your kitchen is getting more agitated as it tries to get outside. You open the window but the fly doesn't recognise the opportunity and remains 'trapped' in the kitchen. Even when you encourage it with the help of a magazine, it ignores your support and goes back to the familiar spot on the pane of glass.

At times, we can be like this fly, unaware of the opportunities we have, ignoring support and wanting to do things the way we always have. Often we continue with the familiar and the comfortable rather than with what works best.

The fly who 'attacks' the window with even more determination, ends up hurt as well as unsuccessful. This is often the case with people who become aggressive and demanding. If we want a different outcome, go for a different approach. Many of us are great at continuing to do what doesn't work, unaware that we have choices.

So what are my choices and indeed what are my current behaviour patterns in conflict?

What's my style?

Whether the tension is about budgets, in-laws, children or sex, people are inclined to respond with pretty much the same patterns. This is usually some form of collaboration, giving in or attacking. Your pattern is likely to take you down a familiar path with each conflict, experiencing the same feelings and getting similar results.

While all styles of dealing with conflict are useful, the best approach depends on the situation you are in and what you want to achieve. There are three main patterns of response:

☞ flight
☞ fight
☞ flow

Develop flexibility if you want to increase effectiveness.

None of these is inherently good or bad, just more or less effective. While flow creates good working relationships and provides a solution to meet everyone's needs, it presupposes the other person wants to collaborate. If not, you may need to protect yourself or use another style to ensure needs are catered for.

Just as a golfer plays with a variety of clubs, you may 'play' the course of human differences better with a variety of approaches. It can be restricting to stay with that club or style which is familiar and comfortable to use.

Flight

Peace at all costs.

Have it your way.

This lose-win style means saying 'yes' to accommodate the other person. It is usually the pattern for people who value the relationship over the goal. Strategically, this may be an appropriate way of responding. For example, you might decide the customer is always right and agree to his request; or you might be with someone who is unreasonable and you decide to accommodate.

However, the lose-win personality (i.e. when it is a consistent pattern rather than a conscious choice), is likely to lead to frustration, anger with self and the danger of being exploited. You can choose flight behaviour without being a flight personality.

Fight

That's a stupid idea.

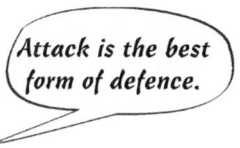

Attack is the best form of defence.

This is the win-lose style. It involves using power, threats, bluffs, intimidation, anything that will help to win the conflict. This pattern is used by people who value goals over relationships.

Again this may be appropriate as a choice in some contexts. When someone vulnerable is being physically or verbally attacked, you may go into fight mode to protect as a first response. This is fight behaviour driven by caring.

When people are not prepared to flow, you may wish to use this approach. For example, you decide to put pressure on an unreliable person to ensure you are no longer inconvenienced by his late reports.

However, the fight personality only values winning, it is 'power over', and has little regard for the person or feelings. This will result in alienation, isolation and resentment. This person becomes 'locked' into win-lose, as opposed to a person who borrows fight behaviour to achieve a particular relationship objective.

Flow

Let's find a way to ...

What can we do to...?

This win-win approach focuses on the concerns of everyone and looks together for ways to reach agreement. This is about standing up for yourself without blaming, accusing, demanding or being hostile. This approach recognises that both sets of needs are important and seeks solutions to satisfy everyone. This leads to win-win, a sense of *power with*, and positive, collaborative relationships.

To flow is non-combative. It is not backing down or burying your head in the sand pretending there isn't an issue. It is going with the energy, the way an Aikido master will flow with the energy of the other rather than fight it. The aim is to divert the attack by disarming the energy. Aikido looks to align and harmonise. In physical practice, it resembles a dance as the attacker's energy is deflected and rendered harmless.

The win-win approach creates partners, not opponents. It means searching for ways to involve and satisfy everyone. The mind set 'let's see how we both can have what is important to us', shows you are not out to fight, it creates that bridge for mutual gain … it is about respect.

While you may need to borrow fight and flight behaviours when the other person is not prepared to flow with you, it is the flow mind set that leads to the sense of collaboration and solutions built from everyone's needs.

Key skills for collaboration

Here are three skills which prevent the escalation of the conflict and allow you to steer the energy along a path that will increase understanding, trust and co-operation.

Successful people are flexible people.

1 *Listen acceptingly* – find out what others see through their window on the world.
2 *Talk constructively* – share what you see through your window on the world.
3 *Problem-solve* – marry the views for mutual wins.

1. Listen to understand the other person's view on the world

To view the difference only from my view will be restricting … I will have limited information. Listening to the other person will provide another view, wider perspectives and more possibilities.

As children, we have been taught to be quiet rather than to listen. Listening means you are open to the other person's perspectives, needs and concerns. It is not judgemental, you accept what the other says as valid and 'right' for them, even if you disagree. It involves putting aside any preconceived notions you may have about that person.

> *Understand first, respond second.*

Listening can be a bit like reading the newspaper. Something catches our eye and we exclude those bits of the paper that are not of interest. We are also inclined to scan and delete as we listen. Quite unconsciously we can listen selectively and filter out information. We don't always hear what is said, and we don't realise this either.

> *Listening is judgement free.*

Checking with the other person that you have heard correctly is a way to build understanding and giving the other person a deeper sense of being heard. Listen to understand and accept, rather than to justify, judge, advise or argue. By listening in this way you are likely to bring out the best in the other person.

Help me to understand …
Tell me about …
Let me see if I understand …
Have I got that right?
Can you give me an example?
How important is this to you on a scale of 0-10?

It is crucial that you listen for what is important to that person. After all, that is why the conflict is happening … because something which is important to that person is being denied. You may just find that it is impossible to continue to be in conflict when someone is trying to understand you and meet your needs.

'Yes buts' indicate argument rather than listening.

Listen for feelings

Feelings can wander around the conversation looking for some acknowledgement to hook on, and once hooked, can somehow fly off and disappear in space. Without validation and air space, feelings can get in the way and block the communication flow.

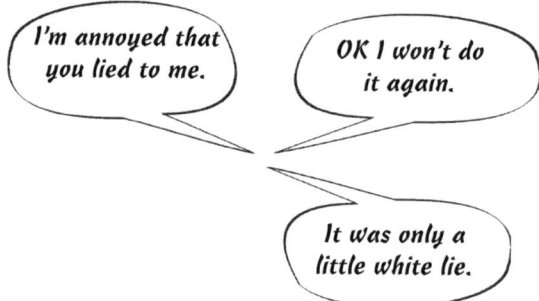

These respond to the substance of what is being said, not the feelings. Here are ways to get the feelings into the conversation.

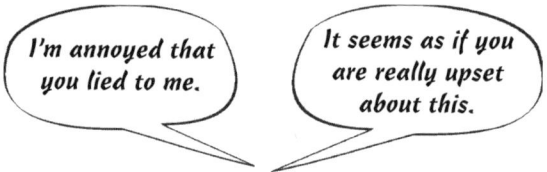

Remember, while you may not agree with the substance of what the other person is saying, you can still acknowledge the importance of feelings. Often, people don't feel listened to until their feelings have been understood.

When Frank says he will spend Sunday afternoon with Susan who feels neglected, he thinks he has not only listened to Susan, but has also dealt with the problem. However, the real issue is her feelings … she needs to have her feelings aired, explored and validated. Only then will she feel that Frank really understands her.

Giving the solution is not always the answer.

Not everyone is like Susan. For some, the solution will be the answer. Give the Franks of this world a 'fix it' approach and understanding to the Susans. Some people will want a mixture of both. People don't always want to be treated in the way you do.

Listen to understand

I feel neglected

There's no reason for you to feel neglected.

What you should do is...

Whilst these reactions may be understandable, they don't deal with the real issue or allow the person to feel understood and accepted. With understanding, the problem often 'melts' away. Incredible as it may seem, 70% of people's problems need no other solution than understanding.

Here are some questions which will help understanding.

What let's you know you are neglected?
What do you need from me so you wouldn't feel neglected?
Help me to understand what it is like to feel neglected.

> Take turns in having equal 'air time'.

How not to do it

Karen:	**I have such a headache. (*explains situation*)**
Samu:	**Do you want a paracetamol? (*wants to help*)**
Karen:	**I've already taken two. (*shares her solution*)**
Samu:	**You try to do too much, why don't you lie down. (*advises with positive intention*)**
Karen:	**I don't want to lie down, I've too much to do. (*rejects the advice – gap widening*)**
Samu:	**That's daft. Anything you have to do can wait. (*justifies advice already given – polarisation begins*)**
Karen:	**Will you stop trying to sort me out. I said I don't want to lie down. (*reacts to advice – gap widens further – resentment*)**
Samu:	**Your problem is you are stubborn, just like your mother. (*accusation – hot button fired – issue widening*)**
Karen:	**And you are a typical male. Just leave me alone and stop telling me what to do. (*stereotyping – feels misunderstood – sense of hopelessness*)**

Karen does not feel listened to and feels annoyed with Samu for giving her advice. Samu feels that not only has he listened to Karen (how could he give advice unless he first listened?) but he has had her best interests at heart. He is feeling confused and hurt as she has rejected his 'help'.

Samu was listening to Karen but not listening to her in a way that would allow her to feel listened to. It is not enough to listen, people must know you have listened.

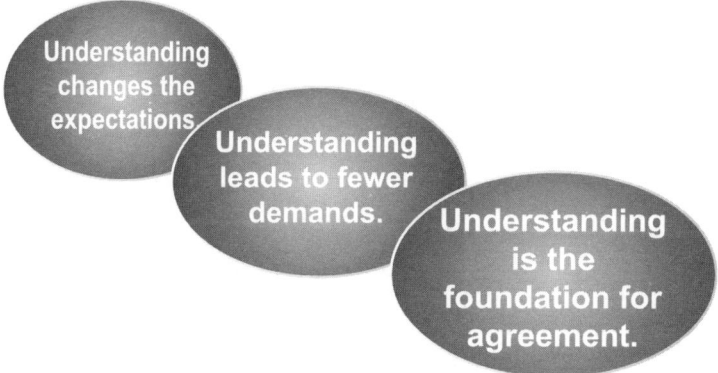

Understanding changes the expectations.

Understanding leads to fewer demands.

Understanding is the foundation for agreement.

Mishearing is the norm

We use words to describe ideas, feelings and needs. But the words are not the experiences, no more than the photo is the person it represents or the brochure is the product it describes. Words are the 'wrapping paper' for our experiences. My wrapper might contain chocolate but you might think it wraps toffee. 'I need more appreciation' might be heard as 'you want a pat on the back' but what I really need are bigger challenges.

It's a pity we speak the same language, because we don't!

What you hear may not be what was actually said. Language is an imperfect way of communicating thoughts and feelings.

For accuracy, check what is inside the wrapper and ask for specifics

> *What specifically do you mean?*
> *In what way, exactly?*
> *Can you give me an example?*

Paraphrasing

Beware of assuming that people hear what you say or that you hear what the other person says. While you hear the words spoken you may not give the meaning to the words that the person intended. George Bernard Shaw said that the problem

Listening gets you into the other person's view.

with communication, is the illusion that it has taken place. Mishearing would appear to be the norm, and then people argue over what was never said. To improve accuracy, let the other person have the floor and every so often sum up in your own words what your have heard. This not only allows you to hear accurately but shows that you are making a serious attempt to understand and get the other's view on the world.

> *So what you are saying is …*
> *What I am hearing is …*
> *Say more about that to help me understand …*
> *Is there anything else you want to say?*

People who say they haven't got time to listen are really saying they don't yet value listening enough to give it the time required. They are also implying they have time for the consequences of not listening, which are misunderstanding, argument and conflict.

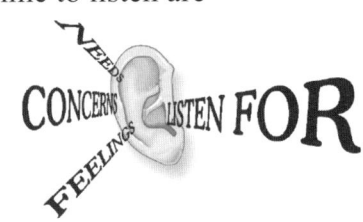

Listening starters

Here are some open questions to get the person talking about the differences. Accompany these with a gentle tone of voice and open body language, so they are heard as invitations to speak.

What are you angry about?
What do you need from me?
What are your concerns?
What needs to happen so it is right for you?
How do you see it?
Say more about why this is important to you.

The voice in your head

Often we can be distracted by what's going on inside … our internal conversation   Sometimes this can be so 'loud' and judgemental it is hard to 'hear' the other person.

There may be plenty you are thinking and feeling but not saying. Aim for a positive internal dialogue which enables you to focus totally on the other person.

Listening makes a lot of sense.

Acceptance listening

1 For the moment, put to one side your concerns, feelings and needs.
   - ☞ Focus on the other person.
   - ☞ Seek his view on the world.

2 Listen for what is important to the other person.
   - ☞ Be genuinely interested.
   - ☞ Encourage her to talk.
   - ☞ Explore her feelings, needs and concerns.

3 Accept what the person says as true for him.
   - ☞ Resist argument.
   - ☞ Suspend judgement.
   - ☞ Recognise his right to say something even if you disagree with it.

4 Every few sentences, sum up what you have heard.
   - ☞ 'So what you are saying is …'
   - ☞ 'What I am hearing is …'
   - ☞ 'Anything else you want to add?'

5 You are not listening acceptingly if you
   - ☞ justify.
   - ☞ argue.
   - ☞ advise.
   - ☞ judge.
   - ☞ interrupt.

Yes quite, but as I was saying …

Yes but …

That's nonsense!

 Rather than create a one way street, drive on a communication highway, where ideas and feelings can pass freely in both directions.

2. Talk constructively to share your view on the world

How do you tell the other person that you feel put upon, misunderstood or that you are hurt and angry? People who are 'honest' in expressing themselves can find it backfires … they end up rowing and further apart. It is not just a question of being honest, you must be honest in skilful ways.

> *'Drawing on my fine command of language, I said nothing.'*
> Robert Benchley

To open with *'I am angry with you because …'*, can be provocative, as the underlying message is 'you are wrong'. Such openings may be how you are viewing the situation but they contain value judgements and imply the other person is at fault.

More openness will be created by acknowledging the differences and seeking to understand the other person's perspective.

> *We seem to have different approaches to …*
> *Help me to understand why you want to …*
> *Would it be a good idea to talk about … ?*

People who talk constructively, express thoughts, feelings and opinions in honest, open and straightforward ways. Remember, you are sharing your view on the world and on this person's behaviour in particular. This is partial, subjective and filtered. It is your opinion and the other person will have a different opinion. You may see the person as a villain. He will see himself as a hero.

> *Avoid character assassination.*

When things don't go right, we're often quick to blame. This is especially true if we have been storing up resentment and anger. Blame the other person and they are likely to blame you.

You only think of yourself.
It's all your fault.

To avoid making the other person wrong, talk about yourself and how that person's behaviour affects you. Using 'I' language rather than 'You' language can prevent the situation getting personal.

Avoid

You are...
You never ...
You should ...
You always ...
You don't ...
You make me feel ...
Why can't you ...

Say

I feel ...
I'd prefer ...
I'd like ...
I need ...
My concern is ...
I don't like ...
I believe ...
As I see it ...

Talking starters

You risk not being heard if you try getting your message across indirectly, through humour or sarcasm. Beware of expecting others to read your mind ... tell people what is important to you and what you need. Here are some sentence starters to enable you to be not only direct but respectful.

I am angry that …
I want …
I am sad that …
I need …
I am sorry that …
I wish …
I am concerned that …
What is important to me is ….
As I see it, what this is really about …

Beware 'Never' and 'Always'

Often we speak in exaggerated terms, especially when feelings run strong.

You never come home on time ...
You always forget to call ...

Does he never come home on time? It might feel he never comes home on time but it probably is an exaggeration. You are likely to be taken more seriously if you make accurate statements or talk feelings: *'It feels as if you never come home on time' 'It feels as if you always forget to call.'*

Instead of saying, *'You are never at home'*, it will be less provocative if you say, *'I feel neglected when we are not at home together.'*

Rather than saying, *'You are always late'* try this: *'When I am kept waiting, I feel unimportant.'*

Try something like, *'When I sense I am excluded from the decision-making process'* rather than *'You never involve me in decision-making.'* 'Always' and 'never' will always (well almost always!) shift the focus away from the real issue. You have created a diversion and probably something else to row about.

Share feelings

Often we confuse being emotional with expressing emotions. You can express emotions well without being emotional and you can be extremely emotional without expressing much of anything.

To say *'I am angry with you because ... '* may provoke a response *'And I am angry with you ...'* with each person getting angrier.

This is happening because people are feeling blamed. It will be more helpful to keep the focus on yourself and what you are feeling. *'I feel angry inside, I'm worried and confused and I need to feel we are at one on this.'*

Talk to the relevant person, not everyone else.

Talk in positive terms

Ever notice how when you go on a diet and you decide not to eat chips and cream cakes ... what do you become obsessed with? Yes, those chips and cream cakes just won't leave your mind.

The mind doesn't seem to be able to handle negatives except as positives e.g. don't think of a pink elephant and what do you get ? How big is your pink elephant!

Beware of saying things which are negative – *'I don't want us to fall out over this'* or *'This is going to be difficult.'* You may just end up getting what you don't want! Keep focused on what you both want rather than on what you don't want. Otherwise it will be like the golfer who says to himself as he is about to strike the ball, *'I don't want to hook the ball.'* The chances are, he will hook the ball precisely because of what he is telling himself. Talk about what you want rather than what you don't want.

Past or future?

It will usually be best to talk about how you want things to be rather than what has led to the present conflict. While accepting that some people need to come to terms with a situation by talking about the past, this can also trigger bad feelings and often leads to arguing, blame and accusation.

Non-verbals

> *Talk future not past.*

Strange as it may seem, your body is part of the conversation. Research indicates that over 70% of any social interaction is non-verbal. Your body, which is never 'silent', communicates attitudes and feelings. This 'commentary' is likely to be 'louder' than the words.

Here are some guidelines to receptive, open body language

1   Look at the person.
   ☞   A stare can threaten.
   ☞   Looking down or away can be interpreted as lacking confidence.

2   Speak in a calm, friendly and controlled tone of voice.
   ☞   Breathe deeply.
   ☞   Avoid mumbling.

3   Match the other person's energy and state.
   ☞   This will aid rapport.

> *Your body is doing a lot of the talking!*

4   Beware the following:
   ☞   arms and legs crossed.
   ☞   hands covering mouth.
   ☞   body facing away from the other person.

If you have a win-win mind set and genuinely want to meet the needs of the other, your non-verbals are likely to automatically communicate openness and receptivity.

Validate

Besides expressing negative feelings, talk about what you appreciate in that person. Recognise the positive intention and what he is trying to achieve. Validate the viewpoint, needs and intention. Say *'I know you are trying to save us money by repairing the washing machine yourself, however I have been without the machine for a week and I need to have clean clothes for the family'* rather than *'This is typical. You can never do anything right. I knew we should have got a service engineer to do the job.'*

RAPPORT

VALIDATE
VALIDATE
VALIDATE
VALIDATE
VALIDATE
VALIDATE

FEELINGS   INTENTIONS

OPINIONS

Interruptions

When someone interrupts you and won't let you finish, you may wish to use some of the following control techniques.

Closing your eyes, putting your hand up and looking away are some non-verbal ways for getting control. It is best to combine these with expressions like *'Please let me finish'* or *'Hear me out.'*

Really, you want the other person not only to hear but to be open to what you are saying. If you first listen to them in non-judgemental ways, you are more likely to be listened to.

Guidelines

Here are some guidelines to enable you express your view on the world and keep a collaborative relationship for win-win.

1   Talk solution rather than problem:
    ☞   Speak about how you want things to be rather than dwell on the past, what has happened, who said what etc.

2   Avoid any hint of blame, judgement or criticism:
    ☞   Beware of words like *'You should ...'* *'You never ...'* *'You make me feel ...'*

3   Talk about what you observe and see rather than what you think or believe:
    ☞   Say *'When talking to you and I don't get eye contact I feel you are not interested'* rather than *'You are not interested.'*

4   Feedback on the behaviours, never the person:
    Talk about the behaviour being a problem for you rather than imply the other is a problem person ... after all the behaviour is not a problem for them.

    Solution pointing rather than finger pointing.

    ☞   no personal comments
    ☞   no mind reading
    ☞   no assumptions

5   Use 'I' language:
    By talking about your truth rather than implying you have the truth you are less likely to appear hostile or accusatory.
    ☞   *'The way I see it ...'*
    ☞   *'My perception is ...'*

6   Offer your support and collaboration:
☞   Make it obvious that you want to be part of the
       solution.

7.   Use feedback to inform:
☞   Beware of using it to advise, blame or demand.

8.   Recognise the positive intention:
☞   Assume the best and give the benefit of the doubt.

*You can be brutally
honest without
being brutal.*

3   Problem-solve for mutual wins

Identify needs

If the listening phase does not lead to a resolution, it will be
necessary to negotiate and problem-solve. The listening is
likely to identify a variety of unmet needs. List these and
decide on one to work with, as it is unwise to work with
several issues at once.

If people don't take time to explore needs they may deal with
wants or symptoms instead of with the root cause. This is a
form of patching things up and leads to continued frustration
and the re-emergence of the conflict in the future.

Brainstorm solutions

List several ways to meet both sets   *Beware of the quick fix.*
of needs on this issue. Aim to get 5
– 10 alternatives. At this stage it is best not to criticise,
judge or evaluate the suggestions … so no 'yes, buts'.
Encourage wacky or way out ideas, anything to keep the
creativity flowing. Evaluation of these ideas will come in the
decision-making phase.

Decide a way forward

Look for what you have in common. Talk about what you agree about. Create a *'yes'* rather than a *'yes but.'* Go through the list and mark anything that both of you are open to. This will narrow the options. Discuss the positives and the negatives of each remaining option. As you talk you are likely to have more choices than was originally thought.

Use currencies in which you both can trade i.e. a win for both of you. You may, in your give-and-take approach, offer things which are easy for both of you to give. Aim for minimal cost and maximum gain. An 'elegant' currency is one which is low cost for one person and is of high value to the other.

View objections as unfulfilled needs.

Agree a plan of action

It is best if this plan is written down and check whether both people understand and agree to it ... who will do what ... how and by when. Being specific can prevent confusion. Set a review date to see how it is working out.

More choices

Beware of the tit-for-tat scenario which only leads to stalemate and lose-lose. If you want people to listen to you, to look for areas of agreement and to meet your needs, first listen to them, look for agreement and seek to meet their needs. While their behaviour is likely to follow yours, there are no guarantees when it comes to people. But generally behaviour breeds behaviour.

How to agree

If you agree with the other person, confirm it by saying what you liked and why you like it, or you may appear patronising.

How to disagree

If you just counter with a different viewpoint without first validating what the other person has said, you may lose rapport and create a *you versus me* situation. Although some people like the directness and don't have an issue with counter-arguing, you are more likely to maintain rapport if you

Agree before you disagree.

☞ validate the idea.

☞ express you reservations.

☞ seek alternatives and problem-solve.

Jeff:	**What I like about your idea is that the report will be shorter (*validate*)**
	What concerns me is that the key sales figures will not be emphasised (*reservations*)
	What can we do so the key sales information is there without making the report longer? (*problem-solve*)

Arguing

Arguing is a poor persuasion technique.

'Yes buts' often indicate argument mode. Arguing is more likely to polarise than to persuade ... people digging their heels in and defending their own positions. People become locked into their own view and are less open to persuasion. If you 'win' the argument, you are likely to have lost the mind and heart and there is no sense of collaboration or understanding. Arguing is win-lose; problem-solving is win-win.

Arguing is a poor persuasion technique as you will be arguing from your own logic and value system. People move for what is important to them, not what is important to you. Make the links to the other person's values, if you want to influence and persuade.

Respond rather than react

Here are some examples of responding positively to concerns and objections. These open questions allow you to reframe the resistance and keep rapport.

It will never work.	**What do you dislike about it?**
My way is better.	**What makes that seem the best option?**
It's impossible.	**What would it take to make it possible?**
I can't.	**What difference would it make if you could?**
You can't do that.	**What would happen if we did?**
That is not the best way.	**What would be the best way for you?**
It's too expensive.	**Compared to what?**

Rules for constructive controversy

Here are some guidelines for keeping the discussion free of blame, accusation and judgement.

☞ Be critical of ideas but not the person.
☞ Listen to understand, not to win.
☞ Recognise all viewpoints as valid.
☞ Be open to new perspectives.

It may be useful to put yourself into the shoes of an observer, someone with no stake in the issue, someone who understands that both sides have valid concerns and can give an objective perspective on moving forward. As this person, what would you say to each of the individuals? How would you comment on their negotiating styles? What would be your suggestions for moving the situation forward?

Not getting what you want can be a wonderful stroke of luck.

Negotiate

1 Listen acceptingly:
   ☞ Show you understand.

2 Look for what you can give to the other person:
   ☞ Meet real needs.
   ☞ Listen to objections and concerns and incorporate these into the agreement.
   ☞ Look for ways to help this person save face.

3 Ask for what you need from the other:
   ☞ Express your concerns and needs.
   ☞ Be prepared to give and take.
   ☞ Look for ways that you can save face.

4 Make it a fair deal:
   ☞ Ensure there is maximum win for both people.
   ☞ Check needs are met.

**The most significant journey
of your life may be to meet
someone halfway.**

Four steps to resolution

While there is more than just one way to resolve any conflict, there are certain processes that will enable you to manage the differences in open and honest ways without damaging the relationship. Here are four steps, using the skills from the previous chapter, that allow you to make the transformation from *you against me* to *us against the problem*. This model has evolved through work on conflict management in organisations and couple counselling.

1 Attend to the other person first.
2 Explore the need behind the want for both of you.
3 Invite the other's solution.
4 Build for maximum win-win.

Step one

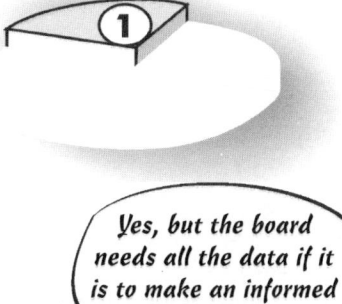

Attend to the other person

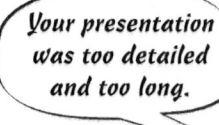

> Your presentation was too detailed and too long.

> Yes, but the board needs all the data if it is to make an informed decision.

When we are criticised or given feedback, the majority of us are likely to justify and explain our actions. After all, we are intelligent people, we have thought out the situation and we do things for reasons.

> The trouble with you is you don't listen.

> But I do listen. Didn't I set time aside on Sunday after lunch so we could talk about the children?

While Frank felt he was listening to Susan, that was not her experience. Frank was not listening to her in a way that allowed her to feel listened to. Justify if you want to start an argument, validate if you want to keep rapport.

Avoid

Lisa: I want to stay out late.

Dad: I want you in by eleven.

Lisa: Yes but all my friends will be out till one o'clock.

Dad: Young lady, what you don't seem to realise is ...

> Beware the 'yes but ...'

Defending yourself, only makes things worse. If, as a first step, you ...

☞ justify
☞ retaliate
☞ explain your situation
☞ talk about what you want

... you are likely to widen the gap and create a barrier. Of course your situation is important. Talk about your situation only after you attend to the other person's viewpoint and feelings. In this way you improve understanding and create a sense of collaboration.

What to do

The first step in resolving conflict is to attend to the other person and validate the opinion, feeling or intention. To validate does not mean to agree. It is the acknowledgement that the person's thoughts or feelings are OK ... it is her reality. For example:

> *What lets you know I don't listen?*
> *How would you want the presentation to be?*

Most of us get locked into our own situation; focus on what we want and need, and are less inclined to consider the other person's needs.

When we have an unmet need, there is pain. The greater the pain, the more we focus on ourselves and our needs. If you lie awake all night with pain from toothache, you know how difficult it is to be altruistic and think of others when you hurt so much. In conflict, there are unmet needs, there is pain ... expect people to focus on themselves. Reverse this if you want to create a collaborative relationship.

Some attending questions

By attending to the other person as a first step, you are likely to minimise resistance, create a feeling of being listened to and begin to build that all important bridge.

> *What needs to happen so it is right for you?*
> *What do you need from me?*
> *What can we do about it?*
> *What would you like to see happen?*

The answer to these questions will tell you what the other person wants, i.e. the solution to his unmet need. If you can meet this solution there will be no need to negotiate or go further on these steps.

Leroy:	You don't listen to me.
Tanya:	What would let you know I listened to you?
Leroy:	Look at me instead of continuing to work on your keyboard.

If Tanya can give Leroy her full attention, then there is a solution which is acceptable to both of them. There is no need to go beyond this step.

Step two

Explore the need behind the want

Lisa wants to be out until one in the morning and Dad wants her home by eleven. They want different things and the wants exclude each other … eleven and one don't go together. Neither of the stated solutions work for the other person.

If Lisa and her dad stay at the level of wants, they will argue, counter-argue, get more frustrated and angry with no progress being made. It will be a *you against me* scenario.

The want or position taken, is seen as a specific solution to a need or interest. Lisa is seeing staying out late as the way to peer approval, and Dad is seeing a return home time of eleven as the way to ensure Lisa's safety.

> **Wants are solutions to needs.**
>
> **Wants often exclude each other.**
>
> **Wants are driven by needs.**
>
> **Needs can be met in ways other than the expressed want.**

Asking a *why* question will flush out the need that is driving the want … Lisa needs to look good in front of her friends and Dad needs to feel she is safe. Peer approval and safety may not exclude each other. At the level of needs both people can problem-solve, negotiate and make real progress.

The win-win for Lisa and her dad might be for Lisa to stay out with her friends and ring him to ensure her safety.

Questions to reveal the need

Unmet needs don't go away.

By exploring the need behind the want, not only will you keep the focus on the other person, you will intensify the feeling of being listened to and deepen understanding.

> *Why is that important to you?*
> *Why does that matter?*
> *Why do you want that?*

Step three

Invite the other's solution

The danger with giving our own solution is that it is designed from our criteria and view of the world and may not match the needs of others. It can be like giving someone your glasses, which have been prescribed for near-sight to someone who suffers from far-sight.

Dad may suggest that Lisa could stay out later provided she uses the mobile phone to keep in touch with him. Lisa may not wish to ring Dad in front of her friends and so dismisses this solution.

Be solution focused

Talk future not past.

Use the *what* question to move from the problem to solution. There is the danger if too much time is spent on the problem, negative feelings will be triggered and a sense of hopelessness created.

Problem-solve on both sets of needs e.g. Dad might ask Lisa, *'What needs to happen so you would look good in front of your friends and yet I would know you were safe?'*

Some problem-solving questions

How would you see us solving that?
What do you suggest?
What would be your solution?
What can we do so you get … (your need) and I get … (my need)?

Inviting the other's solution leads to a sense of *power with* and collaboration. Because the person is involved in designing the solution, you are more likely to get commitment to this rather than compliance.

Step four

Build for maximum win-win

In the same way as you wouldn't knock a wall down in your house without checking why it was built, you may not want to knock an idea without first understanding why it was suggested.

The solution offered may not be as bad an idea as first appears. Madame Curie had a 'bad' idea that turned out to be radium. Richard Drew had a 'bad' idea that turned out to be Scotch tape. It will be useful to recognise the validity of what is offered and then express your concerns. By building on what is offered you can reach an acceptable agreement.

Lisa might say to her dad, *'Look the phone is a good idea, but it'll be naff to be ringing home during the evening. What if I ring you on my way home?'* If this solution does not meet Dad's needs, he may help Lisa to think through the consequences of this suggestion and to negotiate further. The conflict is not resolved until there is a win for both people.

> *What I like about your suggestion is …*
> *My concerns are …*
> *What do you suggest we do?*

Building in this way can not only maximise the win for both people, it can intensify the sense of collaboration and strengthen the relationship.

You against me

Peter:	**Hello James, what can I do for you?**
James:	**I feel I deserve an increase in my salary to reflect my commitment and the hours I've worked in recent months.** (*want*)
Peter:	**We have had a difficult year, sales are down and targets have not being met. Regrettable as it is, I must say no.** (*own situation*)
James:	**Yes but I need more money ... I can't make ends meet.** (*reiteration of position – feels unheard*)
Peter:	**You don't seem to realise – my hands are tied.** (*frustration – feels unheard – gets locked into own position*)

James:	And you don't seem to realise what it's like to scratch a living from the pittance this place pays. (*anger – polarisation of positions*)
Peter:	You are just being unreasonable now. (*accusation*)
James:	And you ... *(slams door)* ... Oh, what's the point? (*gap growing*)

This escalates for the following reasons:

> *Confront the issue not the person.*

☞ Peter's opening response was to explain his situation rather than attend to James and his needs.

☞ The interaction stays at the level of wants ... needs were not explored (I want more money – more money is not available – how many times do I have to tell you).

☞ It is *you against me*. It is '*I want*' versus '*you can't have.*'

The outcome is that neither feels listened to or understood. They are angry and frustrated and the relationship has deteriorated. The issue will smoulder and is likely to resurface some time in the future. A barrier rather than a bridge has been created.

Us against the problem

Peter:	Hello James, what can I do for you?
James:	I feel I deserve an increase in my salary to reflect my commitment and the hours I've worked in recent months. (*want*)
Peter:	If I were to increase your salary, what would that do for you? (*attend – explore needs*)
James:	I would feel my contribution was recognised and I'd feel more valued. (*feels listened to*)

Peter:	So a salary increase would enable you to feel more appreciated. (*feels understood*)
James:	Yes.
Peter:	We've had a difficult year, sales are down and targets have not been met. (*my situation*)
	What can we do so you'd feel more appreciated considering we don't have the money to support a salary increase. (*validation – invite solution*)
James:	I suppose if I was given more responsibility I'd feel more appreciated but I'd still like my salary to be reviewed at the earliest opportunity. (*solution*)
Peter:	If we agree to talk salary in three months time, would that work for you? (*check for agreement*)
James:	Yes.
Peter:	What sort of responsibility did you have in mind? (*focus on other*)
James:	I'd like to head up the next project. (*want*)
Peter:	You certainly have a lot of relevant experience.
James:	I would need …
Peter:	What do you suggest … ? (*build*)

This works because Peter

☞ attends to James as a first step.
☞ flushes out needs.
☞ invites James to give the solution.
☞ builds.

The result of this approach is that James feels listened to and understood, he senses a willingness by management to meet his real needs. He is being taken seriously and his needs are partially met. Although the circumstances are identical in both scenarios – James wants a salary increase and money is not available to support this – a bridge has been built and the relationship strengthened.

Work on the relationship as well as the problem.

Fast track to collaboration

Sheila:	**Your department never produces its reports on time.** (*want*)
Sean:	**It isn't a perfect world. We have problems here I can't always control.** (*justification*)
Sheila:	**Yes but what you don't realise is ...** (*argument*)
Sean:	**And what you don't seem to understand is ...** (*polarisation*)

Of course there are reasons why the reports were not ready. To merely explain why they are not ready is likely to damage the relationship and create *you versus me*.

If you wish to create the collaborative *us against the problem*, include some form of validation and problem-solving. The following example demonstrates how using the third step alone can achieve this.

Sheila:	**Your department never produces its reports on time.** (*want*)
Sean:	**I appreciate deadlines are important,** (*validation*)
	however it isn't a perfect world. We have problems here I can't always control. (*my situation*)

> What can we do to ensure that the inconvenience to you is kept to a minimum considering the fluidity of my situation? (*problem-solve*)

Old habits

> You will create conflict if you do not consider the needs of the other person.

Sometimes you will use these steps while the other person continues in old habits of blame and attack. It can seem as if you are getting nowhere. Even so, it is possible to have a productive discussion:

Naomi: I've been thinking about what happened and I am concerned how it might affect our relationship. I'd like to understand what was going on for you and share my view on things. (*invite*)

Mark: The problem was your attitude, you blindly rush into things. (*attack*)

Naomi: You feel my attitude was unhelpful. (*acknowledge*)

Can you say more about this? (*focus on other*)

Mark: The truth is you shouldn't have said what you did. You make me really angry when you don't think things through. (*accuse and blame*)

Naomi: Sounds like I really got it wrong for you. (*validate*)

What would you have needed from me? (*invite solution*)

Mark:	Well, for a start, I'd like you to …
Naomi:	Why is this important to you?

STEP (2)

Mark:	… (*answer*)
Naomi:	My situation is … what can we do so you get … and I get ….

STEP (3)

As you will probably require the patience of a saint to maintain this process, it may be as well to balance the amount of patience needed against the value of the relationship to you.

Power plays

What can you do with the stubborn person who is dismissive of your needs and is not prepared to compromise? You can be passive, you can fight, or you may wish to confront this person with their behaviour and invite discussion of it.

Here is a way of being assertive while keeping a sense of collaboration. It enables you to begin a conversation without any hint of blame, accusation or demand. It is in three parts:

Never give up on anybody. Miracles happen every day!

1 *The behaviour* – a non-emotive description of the current behaviour
2 *Your response* – how you feel or think about the behaviour
3 *The preferred behaviour* – what you would need instead

> *When I sense my needs are being dismissed*
> *I feel angry*
> *And I would like us to work in more collaborative ways.*

If the other person continues to dismiss your needs e.g. *'You are over-reacting'*, you can loop again on your assertive request.

I appreciate you feel I am over-reacting
However, I feel dismissed
And I would like us to work in a more collaborative way.

This three-part formula is a conversation opener. The discussion is only beginning and it is off to a good start. You still need to explore each other's views and problem-solve for mutual wins.

Real life

Ending a relationship can be an assertive option.

While it makes sense to follow the steps sequentially, a real life conversation is interactive, with people moving up and down and off the steps. The steps are designed so that whatever step you are on, you have access to all the other steps. A productive conversation may require you to go from step one to step three, back to two and so on. Staying on the steps and climbing back on will always be an option!

Language of the steps

View the language given with each step as a suggestion. It may be useful to develop your own style and words while retaining the process.

Let the needs of the other person determine how long you spend on each step. People who come to terms with their problems by talking through their feelings and needing to feel understood, will appreciate delaying on the first two steps. Those who require solutions rather than understanding, will want to move quickly onto the problem-solving stages.

Use the ideas and examples from the previous chapters to help you with this. Paraphrasing can be used with any of the steps to ensure accuracy.

Different styles for different personalities.

Guarantee

The tennis coach does not guarantee you will win your matches after you have had a series of tennis lessons. The coach provides you with more choices and flexibility in your game, increasing the possibility of winning.

Conflict grows in the absence of understanding.

Similarly, these steps do not guarantee a result ... sometimes not only do the wants exclude each other but the needs also. You want space in a relationship, I want intimacy ... compromise may be the only way forward. These steps increase your choices and hence your effectiveness in managing differences.

However the tennis coach can make some guarantees. Hit the ball with a good top spin two feet above the net and the ball will never go over the end line. The guarantee with these steps is that you will manage your differences in open and honest ways without argument or conflict. If you slip into argument or conflict, you have slipped off the steps!

A good relationship requires mutual understanding and acceptance, not always agreement.

Steps for Conflict Resolution

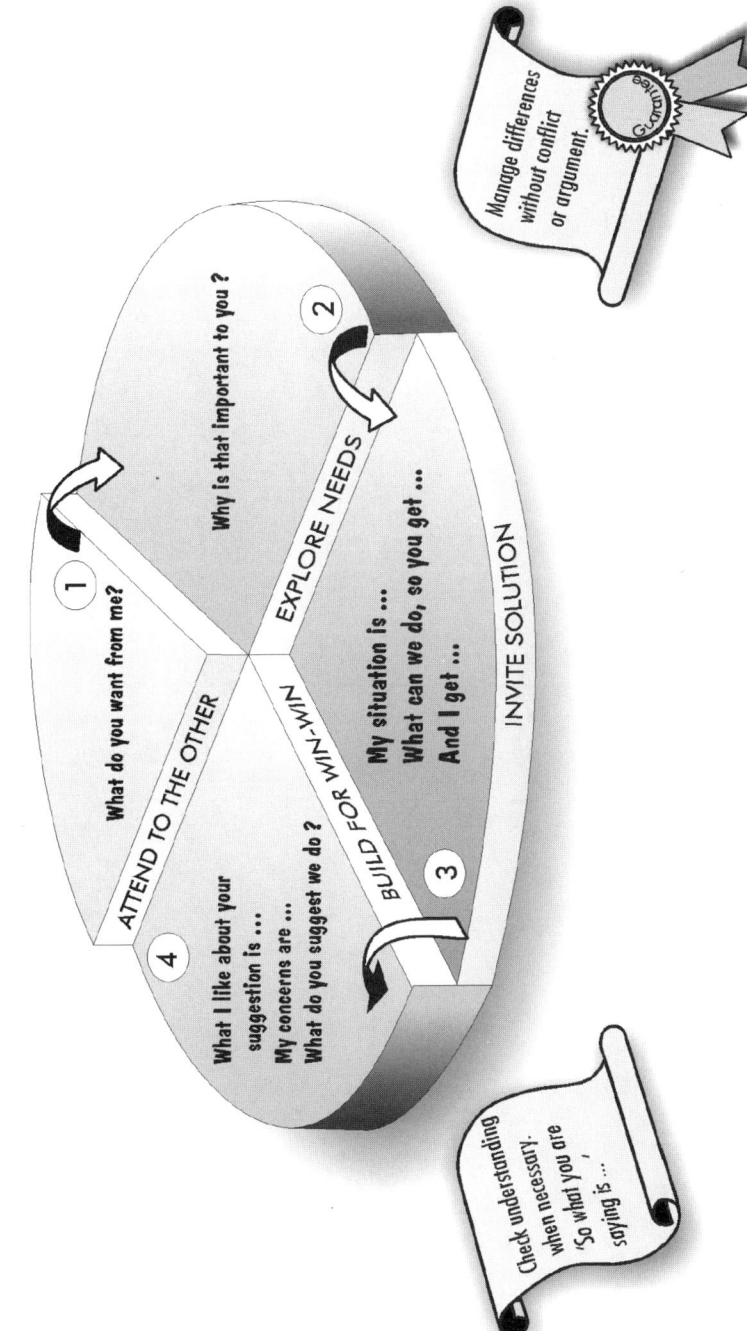

ATTEND TO THE OTHER

① What do you want from me?

EXPLORE NEEDS

② Why is that important to you?

INVITE SOLUTION

③ My situation is …
What can we do, so you get …
And I get …

BUILD FOR WIN-WIN

④ What I like about your suggestion is …
My concerns are …
What do you suggest we do?

Manage differences without conflict or argument.

Check understanding when necessary.
"So what you are saying is …"

Chapter 7
Better Still

Preventing conflict

Rather than wait for the crisis moment before you attend to your relationship, review it when everything is running smoothly. After all, you get your car serviced even though it is running fine. You do this to prevent a breakdown. It's better to visit the dentist for a check up before you get toothache. Grow the relationship when the sun is shining! Take time out for the following:

☞ Review the relationship.
☞ Agree what is going well and what isn't.
☞ Discuss what matters most.

Make quality time

Making quality time for regular discussions can be the best way to clear up misunderstandings. With today's hectic lifestyle it is probably best to set aside some time, which is convenient for both of you, and keep to it. Use the skills to check with each other, giving both of you talking and listening time.

Two views are better than one.

Difficult people

A lot of conflict arises simply because of the assumptions we make about others and the interpretations we put on the things said. Such conflicts could be defused by a few minutes of skilful and honest discussion.

Remember, if you find people difficult, they are likely to find you difficult too. You may want to explore and understand their intention before condemning their actions. Forgiveness is a decision and you may wish to ponder on the question 'Who gains most if you forgive?'

Talk sooner rather than later

Avoid storing up resentment. As soon as you sense discomfort in the relationship, share your concern, even if the cause remains uncertain.

> *I see you as wrong. You see me as wrong. We are both right. That's not logical but it is psychological.*

Pete is becoming increasingly uncommunicative. He comes home from work and wants to be left alone in front of the TV to unwind. Kate feels excluded. The longer she leaves off talking to him, the more the resentment is likely to grow.

Leave it for days or even weeks and Kate will have plenty to say to Pete. *'You never talk to me any more. You take me for granted. All you ever do is work, watch TV and go out with your mates. You are turning out to be just like your father ...'* and it is not likely to stop there!

Had she explained how she felt in the early stages, she wouldn't have been nearly so angry or as willing to blame him. *'Pete, I'm feeling distant from you and I am concerned.'*

People who are good at prevention, see trouble coming and do something about it early. You can stop trouble brewing by recognising the early warning signs and dealing with the minor incidents rather than wait till the full-blown crisis erupts.

Stay current

Avoid broadening the issue by bringing up the past *'You were just like that last Christmas ...'* or mind-reading into the future *'You'll never change ...'* Stay with the present and what you can change now. The past is the playing field of win-lose ... the present is the field of understanding and collaboration. The here and now can be changed. Beware of wasting time fighting over what can never be changed.

Think solutions

Offer a plan for improving things rather than merely complaining or venting your anger. Instead of smouldering because your partner comes home at different times each night and expects supper ready, voice your frustration. Explain that a call just before he leaves the office would solve this problem from your perspective and ask if this would work for him.

Change shoes

Imagine yourself in the other person's shoes. How would it feel to be the other person at this moment relating to you, hearing what you are saying and seeing what you are doing? Swap roles in the argument. Try this in real life and invite your partner to do the same. You might get a laugh by viewing yourself from the other side ... as well as improved understanding.

> *People usually do the best they can with the resources they have.*
> *NLP presupposition*

Avoid the pitfalls

Beware of personalising the problem. If you want help with the washing up, it is unlikely that *'You never help with the washing up'* will make him spring into action. This is a quick way to start an *'I do my share.'* *'No you don't.'* *'Yes I do'* argument.

When you put other person in the 'wrong', the argument can go round in circles and even spirals.

Avoid quick jibes, *'If you call that being together at breakfast, I'd rather you slept in!'* as she slams the kitchen door. Such parting shots can leave a lingering poisonous fallout. Avoid ending a session on a sour note.

If only

Wanting the other person to change is a common 'if only' that most of us have said at some time in our lives.

You are responsible for what you think.

'If only he'd think first.' 'If only she'd stop sulking.' 'If only ... if only.'

This attitude may put you in a passive, victim-like role. You are waiting for the other person to change, to make things all right for you. By sitting around in this passive way you could be waiting a long time for things to improve and you could also be putting your life on hold. The pro active approach is likely to give you more choices and gain respect from the other person.

Playing to the crowd

Open arenas encourage playing to the crowd, taking sides and scoring points.

You are responsible for what you say.

Audiences have their place at sporting events ... in win-lose situations. They don't belong in the arena of understanding. This is best achieved in private.

Name-calling

Insults and name-calling can be baits, drawing you away from win-win. To call someone a nagging bitch or a self-centred egotist is an attack likely to lead to retaliation rather than collaboration.

The impasse

Listen to each other. Show you understand each other. Recognise

You are responsible for what you do.

your needs are not always compatible. Agree to disagree and move on. A good relationship requires mutual understanding and acceptance, not necessarily agreement.

Beware the victim mode

People who whine and nag are less likely to have their real needs met than those who express them openly. Other people cannot read your mind, even though they might try. If you want something badly you may have to come out and ask for it. You may need to replace *'Love is not having to ask'* with *'If I need to feel loved I need to tell you how.'*

Silence is not always golden.

Language suggestions

Unhelpful	Replace with
You should ...	*I need ...*
You are ...	*My perception is ...*
Yes but ...	*Yes and ...*
Who is to blame ?	*What can we do ... ?*

Good luck!

Your relationships today may be where your thoughts and actions of the last few years have brought you. Your future relationships are being shaped by your thoughts and behaviours of today. What you choose to do today affects what you will have tomorrow. Today and now are the places to start. Good luck!

You may not be perfect, neither am I, so we could suit each other admirably.

Alexander Pope

What's Your Style?

Use this questionnaire to discover your preferences in managing conflict.

Imagine real conflict situations and think about how you tend to handle them. For each statement choose the response according to how often you tend to use that way of dealing with conflict.

	Never	Rarely	Sometimes	Often	Very Typical
1 I try to get my own way	1	2	3	4	5
2 I smooth things over and avoid the conflict	1	2	3	4	5
3 I do what is necessary to have my ideas accepted	1	2	3	4	5
4 I try to understand the other person's needs	1	2	3	4	5
5 I let other people have their way	1	2	3	4	5
6 I work with the other person to solve the problem	1	2	3	4	5
7 I fight for my point of view	1	2	3	4	5
8 I walk away from conflict situations	1	2	3	4	5
9 I find a mid point between us	1	2	3	4	5

Transfer your scores from each question onto this grid and then total.

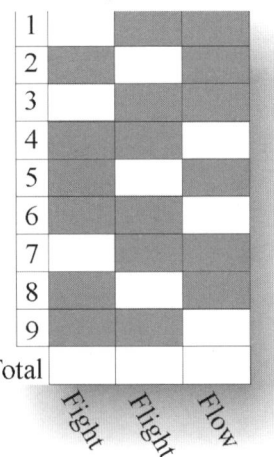

Treat your answers as a rough guide as there will be many variations on these three basic styles. It will be inaccurate to characterise anyone as having a single, rigid style for dealing with conflict. Each of us is capable of using all three styles and indeed, each of the styles will be useful in some situations. See Chapter 5 for a full explanation.

Resolution Route

Handling Accusations

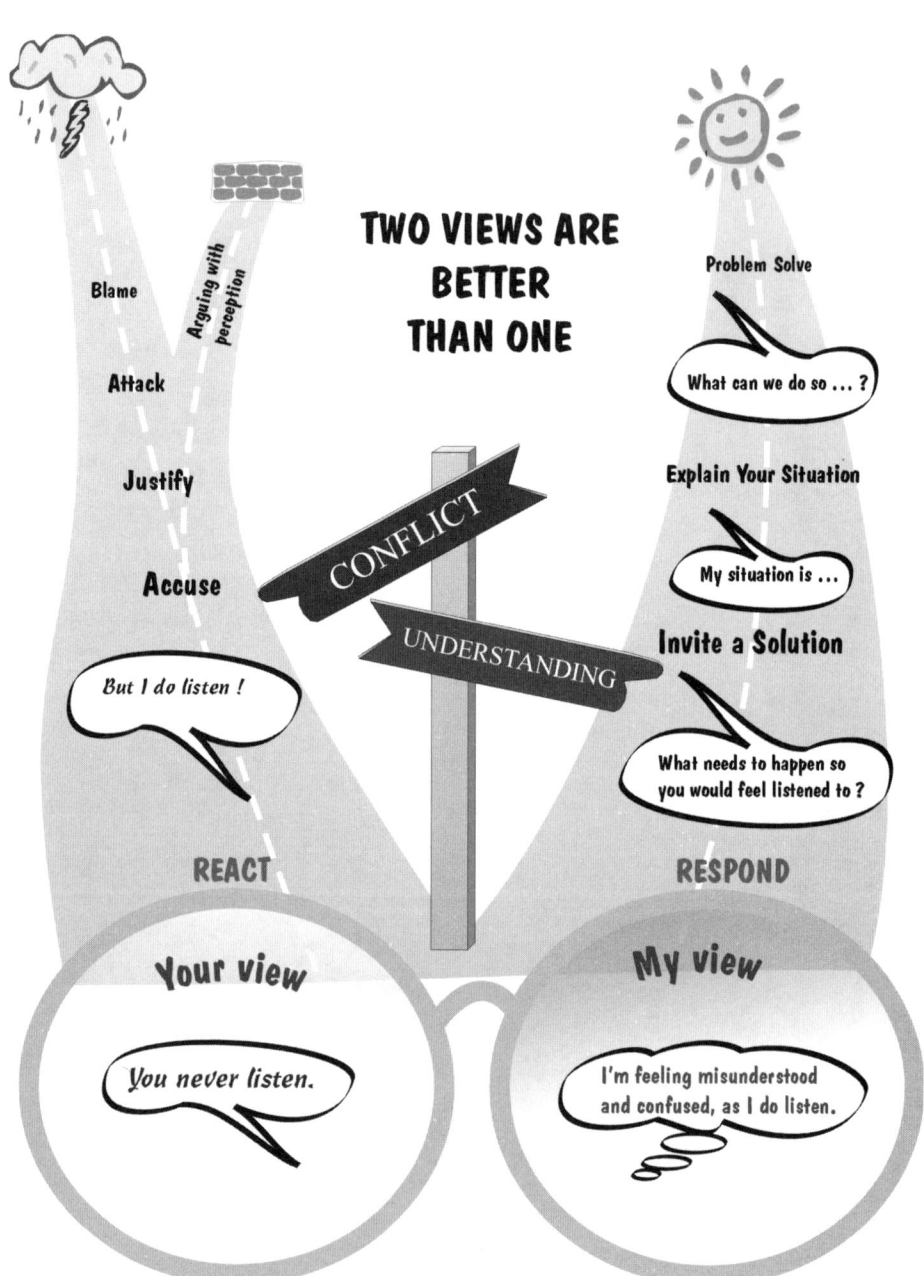

Group Conflict

The more people involved in a conflict, the more complex it will be to meet everyone's needs.

Complete a segment for each individual involved in the conflict and negotiate to an agreed solution, which is to be built from everyone's needs. This sheet is suitable for four people.

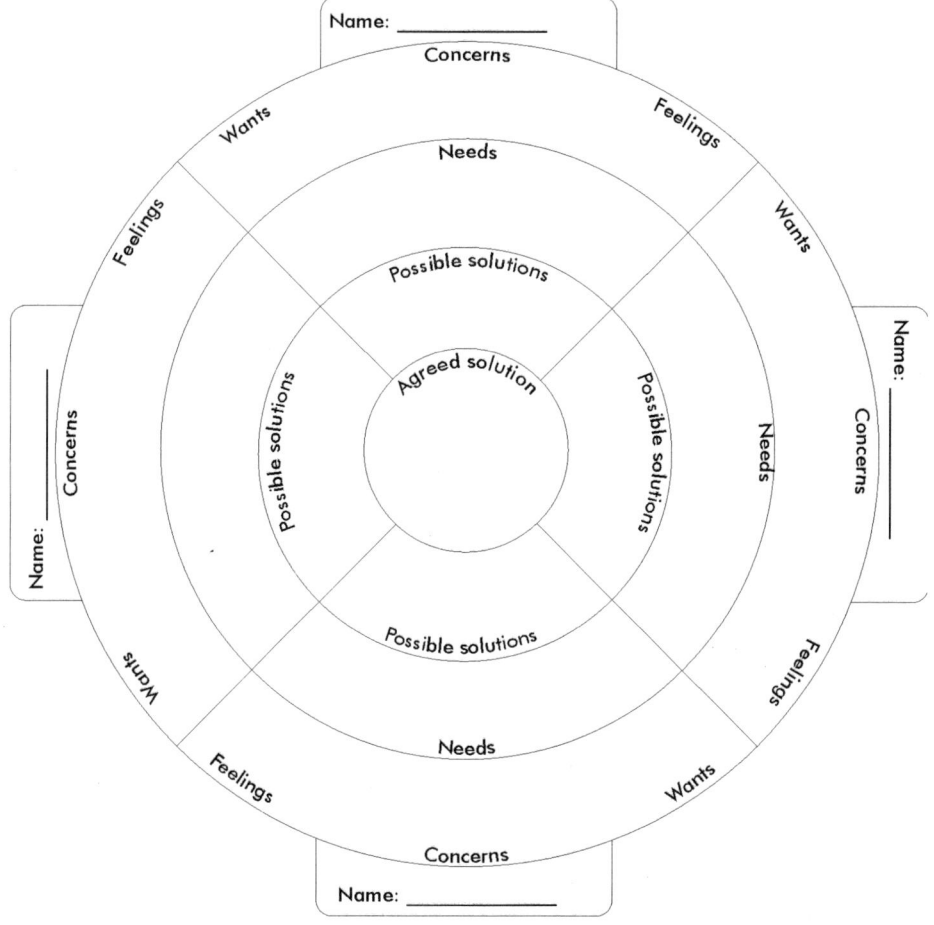

**Start from the point of agreement
rather than the disagreement.**

Listen and Talk

LISTEN ACCEPTINGLY

1 For the moment, put to one side your concern feelings and needs.

2 Listen for what is important to the other person
   ☞ feelings – concerns – needs

3 Accept what the other person says *as true* for him
   ☞ resist argument
   ☞ suspend judgement

4 Sum up what you have heard every few sentences
   ☞ *So what you are saying is ...*
   ☞ *What I am hearing is ...*
   ☞ *Anything else you want to add?*

5 You are not listening if you
   ☞ justify – argue – advise – interrupt

TALK CONSTRUCTIVELY

1 Talk about what you
   ☞ are feeling
   ☞ are concerned about
   ☞ see as your real needs

2 Use 'I' language
   ☞ *I feel ...*
   ☞ *My concerns are...*
   ☞ *What I need is ...*

3 Beware
   ☞ accusation – *You are always ...*
   ☞ blame – *You make me feel ...*
   ☞ demand – *You should ...*

At a Glance

Meeting

Growing a Barrier

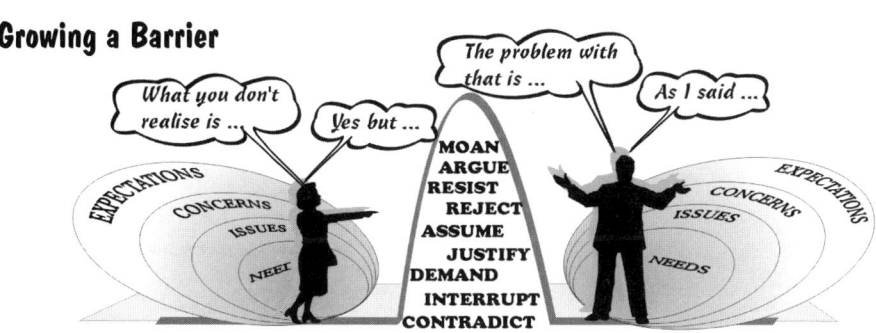

Digging Yourself Into a Hole

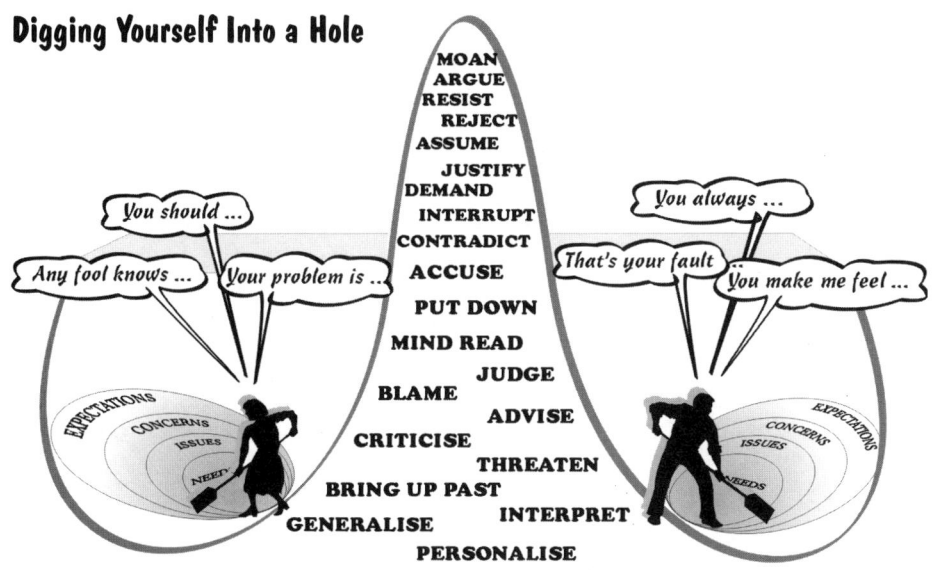

The Wider Picture

The higher you climb,
the more you'll see,
the broader the perspective,
the clearer the areas for agreement.

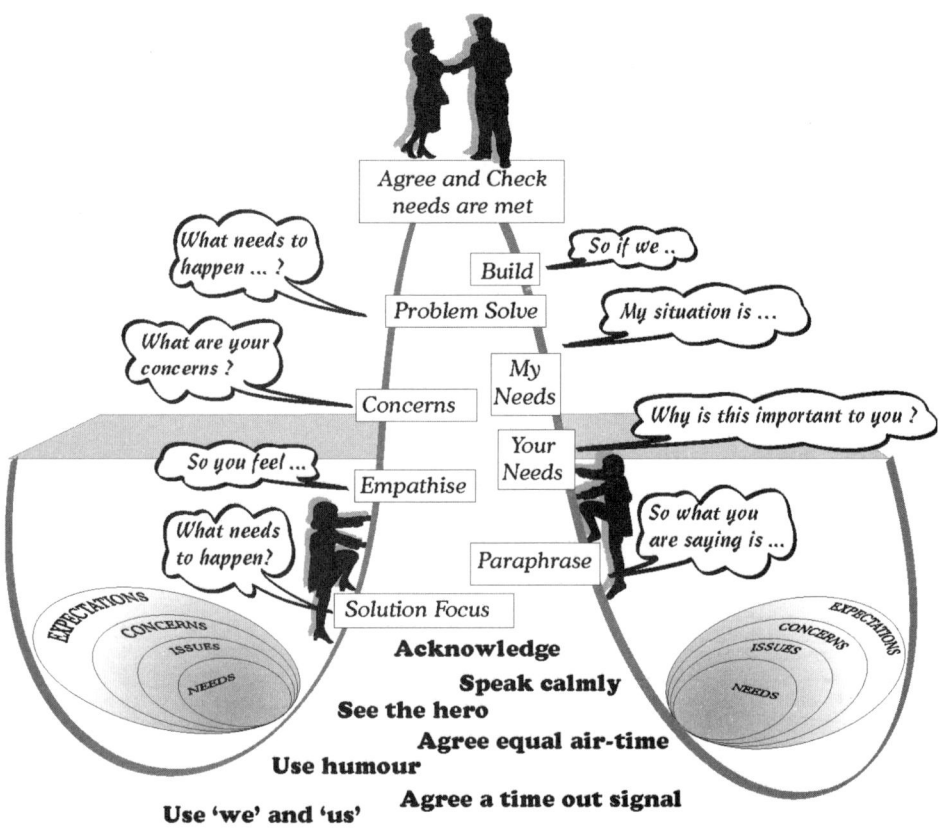

Rather than argue, problem solve on
both sets of needs.

You and I

I explain quietly. You
listen without judgement. You
hear my needs. I
feel my wounds healing.

You see both sides. I
feel understood. I
reciprocate. You
sense my sharing.

I am dove. You
recognise my fear. You
offer an olive branch. I
feel your love.

You cry. I
wipe your tears. I
reach out. You
and I embrace.

With apologies to
Roger McGough.

Bibliography and further reading

Bolton R. *People Skills* Prentice-Hall 1986

Booher D. *How to Say it Right First Time* McGraw-Hill 1994

Cornelius H. and Faire S. *Everyone can Win* Simon Schuster 1989

Covey R. *The 7 Habits of Highly Effective People* Simon Schuster 1989

Dana D. *Talk it Out* Kogan Page 1990

Elgin S. *How to Disagree without being Disagreeable* John Wiley 1997

Stone D. Patton B. Heen S. *Difficult Conversations* Michael Joseph 1999

Quinn M. & T. *Couple Alive* Family Caring Trust 1998

Ury W. *Getting Past No* Business Books Ltd 1991

For more information on People First and the range of products and workshops contact

Tel: (+44) (0) 1425612610   www. peoplefirst.cjb.net

NOTES

NOTES